# THE SONNETS OF
# ANDREAS GRYPHIUS

# THE SONNETS OF ANDREAS GRYPHIUS

## Use of the Poetic Word
## in the Seventeenth Century

Marvin S. Schindler

*UNIVERSITY OF FLORIDA PRESS* ᪉ *1971*
*GAINESVILLE*

*A University of Florida Press Book*

BOOK DESIGN BY STANLEY D. HARRIS

*Library of Congress
Catalog Card No. 79-630254
ISBN 0-8130-0301-6*

MANUFACTURED FOR THE PUBLISHER BY
STORTER PRINTING COMPANY, INC.
GAINESVILLE, FLORIDA

To DAN, LORE ELAINE, and INGE-MARIE
with the hope that they remember, however,
that not books or authors but only people
are the important thing

# Preface

It would seem that to most students of literature (except for the specialist in German literature) the poetry of Andreas Gryphius still remains something of an unknown quantity in spite of the fact that he is clearly one of the great poets of seventeenth-century Germany. Those whose primary concern is with French or English literature of this period, for example, are not likely to be familiar with the man or his works, although it is safe to say that his English and French counterparts are well known to the Germanist. Part of the reason no doubt lies in the fact that the literature of which his is so outstandingly representative has long been considered primarily derivative. Even for the Germanist, however, with the exception of several notable articles in recent years, little has been published in the way of thorough explication and interpretation of Gryphius' poetry. No book on the poetry has ever appeared in English. It is hoped that this short study may be a beginning.

I am indebted to the University of Virginia Committee on Summer Grants, whose generous research fellowship in 1968 allowed me to devote that entire summer to the writing of this book, and to the University of Virginia Committee on Research Grants for a supplementary stipend in 1968–1969 to cover incidental expenses.

To my former teachers, advisors, and colleagues who contributed so much time and interest to me while I was their student and later during the planning and preparation of this book I owe a debt which is impossible to repay. It is the custom at this point, however, to attempt the impossible with a brief acknowledgment, even though it cannot suffice. My sincere thanks, then, to the following persons: Professors Hugo Bekker, Dieter Cunz, Wolfgang Fleischhauer, and Oskar Seidlin, all of Ohio State University; and Professor Walter Naumann, Technische Hochschule, Darmstadt. If this book has at all succeeded, the reason lies with them; if it has not, they bear none of the responsibility.

I am indebted also to the *Modern Language Quarterly* for permission to reprint parts of my article, "Interpretations of 'Es ist alles eitel': The Changing Face of Gryphius Criticism," which appeared in that journal in June, 1967. A portion of chapter 7 originally appeared in *The Germanic Review* (May, 1970) and is reprinted here with permission.

Finally, my thanks to my wife Pat and to my typist Barbara Williams, both of whom remained relatively cheerful in spite of it all.

*June, 1970*                              MARVIN S. SCHINDLER

# Contents

## Part I
## The Poetic Word: An Evaluation

## Part II
## The Biblical Word as the Poetic Word

# PART I

## The Poetic Word
### An Evaluation

# 1

# Introduction

Although Andreas Gryphius is generally cited in histories of German literature as the outstanding poet of the seventeenth century, and probably rightly so, surprisingly little scholarly work has been devoted to a close examination of his lyrics. When we consider the body of literary criticism in modern times, it is certainly fair to state that, despite the much heralded resurgence of interest on both sides of the Atlantic in the German literary Baroque, we have hardly been overwhelmed in the past sixty-five years by a deluge of books and articles concerned with Gryphius' poetry. Even the three-hundredth anniversary year of his death, 1965, while notable for the appearance of the first volumes of the long-awaited new critical edition of his works, was not marked by an unusual amount of Gryphius scholarship. Writing in 1957, Hugh Powell, the distinguished Gryphius scholar, lamented this dearth of critical activity and proposed some new directions for future research. In his specific suggestions of fruitful areas, Powell pointed out that much still remained to be done on the development of Gryphius' lyric style, a subject particularly rich in possibilities because of the fact that the poet often revised his poems painstakingly and extensively for the several editions printed during his lifetime: "Was wir bereits sagen können ist, daß die Verbesserungen dazu dienten, die Lebendigkeit und Klarheit der Sprache und die Ausdruckskraft des Rhythmus zu vergrößern. Aber die eindeutige Bestimmung der Bedeutsamkeit des Rhythmus in Gryphs Lyrik steht noch aus." ("This much we can say already—that the revisions served to increase the vitality and clarity of the language and the expressive power of the rhythm. But the real determination of the significance of the rhythm in Gryphius' lyric poetry still remains to be made.")[1] Such a tentatively positive evaluation of Gryphius' revisions and the purpose they served, reasonable as it may seem, was little short of revolutionary. It is likely that the subsequent failure to mine this neglected ore was due in large part to a critical view of the nature of Gryphius' poetry—indeed, of seventeenth-century poetry in general—which, exhibited long before the date of Powell's article, had by then already solidified. As a result, such matters were considered sufficiently treated. In addition, Powell indicated that the question of the influence upon Gryphius of such older contemporaries as Johann Heermann, Valerius Herberger, and Johannes Plauen had still to be answered satisfactorily, and that a study of Gryphius' religious poetry was sorely needed. Only in 1965 did a single article on the *Sonn-und Feiertagssonette* appear.[2]

Few interpretations of individual poems have been published since the turn of the century, a situation which is probably due to some extent in recent years to the hesitation of students of the so-called intrinsic method to approach the poetry of this period, which has long been labeled stylized and devoid of originality, even in its best poets. Nor have there been many substantial studies of Gryphius' poetry as a whole from a wider perspective. Not a single book has appeared in English. Indeed, until just two years ago, only three larger works that treat the poetry extensively could be counted in this century: Victor Manheimer's pioneering *Die Lyrik des Andreas Gryphius*, in 1904; in 1933, Gerhard Fricke's *Die Bildlichkeit in der Dichtung des Andreas Gryphius*; and, in 1959,

1. "Probleme der Gryphius Forschung," *Germanisch-Romanische Monatsschrift* n.s. 7, o.s. 38 (1957): 339. This and all subsequent parenthetical translations are the author's unless otherwise noted. The renderings are intended as prose translations, although an attempt has often been made to retain the original meter.
2. Hans-Henrik Krummacher, "Andreas Gryphius und Johann Arndt. Zum Verständnis der 'Sonn- und Feiertags-Sonette,'" in *Formenwandel. Festschrift zum 65. Geburtstag von Paul Böckmann*, ed. Walter Müller-Seidel and Wolfgang Preisendanz (Hamburg, 1965), pp. 116–37.

Marian Szyrocki's *Der junge Gryphius*. But certainly more disturbing than the paucity of critical studies has been the rigidity of the viewpoint of most of the existing and authoritative major works. Although there may be a slowly growing dissatisfaction with the tenor and methods of the accepted Gryphius scholarship to date, the opposition is as yet isolated, and there has been no widespread general attempt to reconsider the traditional methods and make use of new approaches.[3]

Manheimer's book is properly recognized as the first modern breakthrough in Gryphius criticism. Followed for many years by a silence that indicated the apparent acceptance of its arguments, it has, in all likelihood, exerted more influence on later Gryphius investigations than any other single work. This influence, however, has been so complete that Manheimer's conclusions have never been seriously questioned. Indeed, many of the weaknesses of the later interpretations stem from the fact that these early opinions passed unchallenged and filtered through to more recent Gryphius scholarship; there, by both tacit acceptance and explicit support, they have gained more and more the stature of authority which is *not* to be challenged—an authority which, if we are honest, is at least partly undeserved. To Manheimer we owe the discovery of the hitherto unknown *Lissaer Sonettbuch* of 1637. The earliest publication of German sonnets by Gryphius, it contains thirty poems, many of which were very extensively revised for later printings and thus offer an excellent opportunity for tracing the development of the poet's style. Besides these sonnets, he included his own comprehensive list of corrections to the Hermann Palm edition of Gryphius' poems plus additional variant readings. In the main sections of the text, Manheimer is primarily concerned with the external aspects and the mechanics of the lyrics. Whether he is discussing the avoidance or use of various rhetorical devices, specific images, or poetic phrasing, whether he deals with matters of syntax, meter, or grammar, he stresses always the poet's alleged inflexible adherence to the Opitzian conventions of his day. By comparing the original and revised versions in some cases, and by contrasting the technique and style of earlier and later poems,

3. Articles such as that by Günther Weydt, "Sonettkunst des Barock," in *Jahrbuch der deutschen Schillergesellschaft* 9 (1965): 1–32, in which the author differs strongly with the prevailing opinion concerning Gryphius' revisions, are still relatively rare exceptions.

Manheimer describes what he considers a process of development in Gryphius' lyric—an almost exclusively negative development, by most current standards—from which the poet emerges as a narrow conformist who is willing to sacrifice any and all poetic values, provided that such sacrifice enables him to comply with the formal rules of the poetics for poetry-making. Although the extent of Manheimer's compilations remains impressive today and his statistics are undoubtedly reliable, his critical judgments on the poetry should long ago have received closer attention.

Fricke's study became the second major piece of literary criticism to deal at length with the poems. After a discussion of the function of imagery according to seventeenth-century poetics, he closely examines the individual images and metaphors which appear in Gryphius' lyrics, arranging them into groups and subgroups under the two general headings of *Stoffgruppen* and *Bedeutungsgruppen*. Throughout these listings and also in the related essays that make up the last section of the book, he contributes critical commentary on the goals and functions of the individual images, the reason for their selection by the author, and the use of imagery in general by Gryphius. There is much of the same emphasis found in Manheimer on the formula and the lack of the personal. Fricke further stresses the artificial and the decorative elements in the poetry, which is in his eyes hardly more than the product of a mechanical process, an intellectual game, with words as counters, that works through the arbitrary selection of images and metaphors from existing compendia at the disposal of all poets. This selection is, then, made without regard for the unity of the poem as an artistic whole. Because of the poets' indifference to or even active attempt to exclude subjective factors, seventeenth-century poetry, insofar as it actually remains a process of creation from linguistic material, becomes for Fricke an objective occupation of the intellect. Poetic images are realized, not when their source lies in the individual poets' subjective impressions, but when they are intended to represent the general, the objective, the intellectually meaningful. Thus Fricke speaks of the role of subjectivity in Baroque poetry: "Diese Kategorie der Subjektivität, die im 18. Jahrhundert zur selbstverständlichen Voraussetzung der Dichtung, des ästhetischen Vorganges wird, bleibt im 17. Jahrhundert, wenigstens in der zur Erörterung stehenden Literaturgeschichte ausgeschlossen. Hier ist das Ich des Dichters wie des Lesers als das Willkürliche, Belanglose ausgeschaltet." ("This category of subjectivity, which is to become the obvious prerequisite for poetry—for the esthetic process—in the eighteenth century, is still excluded in the seventeenth century, at least in the history of literature under discussion here. Here the poetic 'I,' like that of the reader, is omitted as something arbitrary and insignificant.")[4] And Fricke leaves no doubt that what is here stated in more general terms must be held valid for Gryphius also.

Although Fricke himself had intended his examination to be only a first step, for many years it seemed likely to become the final chapter as well as the introduction to Gryphius' use of imagery. The few dissertations in Germany which followed it offered on the whole no new insights, and shorter works and articles appeared only seldom. Not until 1959 did Szyrocki, who later collaborated with Powell on the new Gryphius edition, publish the first important work on the poetry in more than twenty-five years. For the first time since Fricke, the matter of imagery was treated in some detail. More remarkable is the fact that for the first time since Manheimer an attempt was made to find the motives behind the poet's revisions and to evaluate them. Szyrocki's main contribution, however, probably lies in his discussion of number-mysticism in the poems of the young Gryphius; when he elsewhere treats the poetry in general or interprets individual poems, his arguments and methods, for those who know Fricke and Manheimer, sound more than a little familiar. Finally, in 1966, Dietrich Walter Jöns presented a new attempt to determine the substance of Gryphius' poetry.[5] If Fricke, with his eyes fixed on the Age of Goethe, emphasized the great distinctions between Baroque allegory and eighteenth- and nineteenth-century symbol, Jöns, looking backward, is concerned mainly with establishing a clear continuity by stressing largely the emblematic features of Gryphius' imagery and placing it firmly within the Christian-allegorical tradition of literature that works by analogy. The fact that Jöns takes issue with Fricke on several of the latter's more extreme judgments is in itself a healthy sign, and no one can deny the relevance of the vogue of emblem writing and its connection in theory and practice to seventeenth-century poetry. However, despite an enormous amount of apparently substantiating

4. *Die Bildlichkeit in der Dichtung des Andreas Gryphius* (Berlin, 1933), p. 197.

5. *Das "Sinnen-Bild." Studien zur allegorischen Bildlichkeit bei Andreas Gryphius* (Stuttgart, 1966).

documentation and occasional brilliant insights, Jöns' viewpoint is itself rather too narrow and confining.

This investigation, which comprises the analysis and interpretation of several Gryphius sonnets, developed from the consideration of a single sonnet within this group, "Es ist alles eitell," and my subsequent disagreement with the existing evaluations of this frequently examined poem. When it became clear that the divergence of views was not restricted to one single sonnet, but was a reflection of more far-reaching differences of opinion, ultimately concerning the general method of approaching Gryphius' lyric, the original essay was extended to its present form—a close analysis of what I consider to be a representative, though small, group of sonnets. The result is, however, not simply a compilation of negative criticisms, an attempt to contradict earlier critiques; rather, I hope that each of the interpretations that follow can stand on its own merits and that together they make some positive contribution to the already existing material on Gryphius. I should like to make clear at the outset that no comprehensive study of Gryphius as a lyric poet, no general survey of the author and his work, is intended. Such an undertaking would need to go far beyond the scope of this exploration of a very few poems. Although the book is composed mainly of individual interpretations, each of which can be read separately, the selection of the sonnets has not been completely arbitrary, nor are the analyses so isolated from one another as might at first glance seem to be the case. As I have pointed out above, Manheimer, Fricke, and Szyrocki, certainly the three foremost Gryphius scholars of this century, have dealt extensively with the poet's use of imagery, techniques of revision, and rhetorical devices. All three have, I feel, oversimplified these matters enough to warrant a re-examination.

The first part of the book is devoted to such a re-examination of four sonnets—"Es ist alles eitell," "Auf die Geburt seines ältesten Sohnes Christiani," "Über die Geburt Jesu," and "Abend." All four of these poems are well known and have been analyzed or referred to in the critical literature. All four are also linked by different aspects of a complex of themes centering on the concepts of time and transience. As a result, they contain some of the most significant ideas and images to be found in Gryphius' poetry. Another conspicuous element of the first sonnet "Es ist alles eitell"—the biblical sources of so many of its images and phrases—led directly to the composition of the second part of this study, which deals primarily with poems selected from the two books of *Sonn-und Feiertagssonette*. These two cycles of one hundred sonnets have largely been ignored by most Gryphius research or, as in the case of Manheimer, they have been dispatched as the insignificant harvest of a temporary influence of such men as Heermann and Herberger on Gryphius—the trivial and poetically uneventful imitative efforts of an impressionable young poet. To my knowledge, none of the three sonnets I have chosen has been discussed thoroughly before. Nor are they very obscure poems; their customary inclusion in modern anthologies of seventeenth-century German verse testifies to that. Each of the three poems draws its theme from a different type of biblical report about Jesus: a parable told by him, a significant event in his life, or an account of one of the healing miracles told of him. The final chapter, which treats a group of poems with religious themes from the second book of sonnets, inquires into the possibility of a relationship between the practice of meditation and the writing of poetry as a key to Gryphius' style.

Gryphius scholarship has suffered in the past, not only from the rigidity of the critical posture manifested in the works of its main representatives, but also from an excess of a curiously applied type of biographical criticism that betrays an attempted reliance on really inapplicable criteria for *Erlebnisdichtung*. In addition, a marked tendency to work down deductively from the precepts of seventeenth-century poetic theory itself and the modern generalizations of *Geistesgeschichte* to the individual poems very likely has done more harm than good. For all of this has tended to draw attention away from the poetry itself. A great deal of time has been spent, for example, in conjecture about the person of "Eugenie" and in the arrangement of the sonnets dedicated to "her" into a chronological order which would help to prove the existence of a real, flesh-and-blood Eugenie. Gryphius scholars have attempted thus to prove her identity as Elizabeth, the daughter of Gryphius' patron Schönborner. The next step has been to use this imagined actual sequence of the poems to support the "facts" of her alleged unhappy love affair with the poet. The critics have devoted very little attention, however, to a serious analysis of these poems themselves. Similarly, it is apparently Szyrocki's positive evaluation of the young Gryphius' supposed greater emotional involvement in the creation of his poems and the resulting "direct" translation of feeling into poetry which, in his selection for the new critical edition, tips the scales in favor of the earliest complete version of each poem rather than the more customary choice from the *Ausgabe letzter Hand*. His brief statement on the relative merits of the original over the revised version of the sonnet "Es ist alles eitell," which is included in the introduction to the first volume of the poems,[6] appears in greater detail in *Der junge Gryphius*. Essentially, in this book, Szyrocki maintains the superiority of the original over the revised poems on the basis of the greater naturalness and intensity of feeling displayed in the former; an aura of personal involvement and subjective expression, compared with a claimed artificiality and coldness; and a yielding to the forces of convention and the emerging dominance of the impersonal, both of which take their toll in the latter. I shall discuss his comments and the validity of such an approach when the sonnet most directly concerned is re-evaluated in the first chapter of this study.

The interpretations of the following pages attempt to focus attention primarily on the poems themselves and are based upon several fundamental beliefs concerning literary criticism in general and the literary Baroque in particular. I shall disregard the entire question of the "truth" of a poem as supposedly determined by the degree and extent of the poet's emotional relationship to his work. Similarly, I must regard the question of whether poet or poem is sincere, that is, of whether a given work of art is the result of the poet's true feelings or is the direct expression of such feelings, as irrelevant and inadmissible to the discussion of a poem, insofar as the presence or absence of such "genuine" feeling is considered in itself a valid evaluative criterion. Rather than burden the analyses—and the reader—with extraneous assumptions as to whether the poet really means what he says or is merely reacting in the only way possible to prevailing literary theory and tradition, I shall try to analyze the poems from within. The point is an important one, especially for the seventeenth century, whose poets, living in an age when the individual artistic personality is alleged to have been sacrificed to the norm of the poetic, have often been charged with the use of imagery which is merely decorative, often

---

6. *Andreas Gryphius. Sonette,* vol. 1, ed. Marian Szyrocki, in *Andreas Gryphius. Gesamtausgabe der deutschsprachigen Werke,* ed. Marian Szyrocki and Hugh Powell (Tübingen, 1963 ff), ix–x. Unless otherwise noted, citations from Gryphius in the text are from this edition, indicated as *Werke.*

stale, and frequently redundant. The images, it is said, tend to be lifeless and empty because they are unfelt and impersonal, usually extracted from vast storehouses of well-sorted, ready-made, multi-purpose word pictures, rather than the original inventions of each author for particular and perhaps exclusive use in a given poem. I shall be concerned primarily with the statements made by the poems themselves, more with how Gryphius employs certain meta-phors than with which metaphors he uses or who has used them before. I proceed on the assumption that there is no one-to-one equation between the originality of an image, the authentic mani-festation of the poet's innermost feelings, and the relative merits of the resulting poem. The success or failure of a poem, its fundamen-tal greatness or lack of it, cannot be related to or explained by any fanciful conviction concerning sincerity or warmth of feeling as subjectively sensed by a given reader. As René Wellek and Austin Warren have argued, the term itself is so ambiguous when applied in literary criticism as to preclude its use as a justifiable criterion for evaluation: "As for 'sincerity' in a poem: the term seems almost meaningless. A sincere expression of what? Of the supposed emo-tional state out of which it came? Or of the state in which the poem was written? Or a sincere expression of the poem, i.e., the lin-guistic construct shaping in the author's mind as he writes? Surely it will have to be the last: the poem is a sincere expression of the poem."[7]

It may well be that, as Bernhard Blume puts it succinctly in a discussion of Rilke, any attempt to interpret a poem must contend with two basic opposing and individually equally unfulfillable demands on the interpreter: that of the theory of *werkimmanenter Deutung*, which insists that a given poem be considered in a vacuum and that the means for its full comprehension by the reader lie within the poem itself, and that of a method which denies with equally strong conviction that it is possible to com-prehend completely any work of literature unless that work's rela-tionship to the entire body of world literature and literary tradition and, often as well, to biographical or other extraliterary data is called upon as an aid to understanding and interpretation.[8] The

7. *Theory of Literature* (New York, 1949), p. 215.
8. "Rilkes 'Spätherbst in Venedig,'" in *Interpretationen I. Deutsche Lyrik von Weckherlin bis Benn*, ed. Jost Schillemeit (Frankfurt am Main and Hamburg, 1965), pp. 277–90. For another view, cf. Sigurd Burckhardt, "Zur Theorie der werkimmanenten Deutung," in *Festschrift für Bernhard Blume*,

two methods, however, cannot be considered as mutually exclusive or as working at cross purposes. It is difficult to avoid the fact that poetry, by the very nature of its art form, *is* by *saying*, and that what a poem says and how it says it both determine its success or failure. We must, necessarily, find these determinants only within the poetic construct itself. Once it is agreed that the ultimate value of a poem is intrinsic in it, then it must follow that such matters as the poet's own emotional rapport with it cannot be considered meaningfully in an interpretation of, or judgment on, that poem.

The concern of interpretation of poetry, then, is to discover those laws which govern, shape, and form a poem by organizing, relating, and integrating all its parts, all its facets, into a cohesive whole—that is, to discover what it says, how it says it, and what there is within the poem that enables it to *say* in that peculiarly unique manner which sets it off from ordinary discourse. The social, political, and language structure of the period in which a poem is written, the religious and general philosophic views of the author, the tradition in which he writes and from which he doubtless borrows, the inescapable fact of the existence of earlier and later versions of specific poems—it would be foolish to suggest that such factors, external though they be, cannot possibly be useful for the understanding of poetry. Their role, however, is that of the footnote—to clarify and to explain. The meaning and worth of the text remains within the text itself. One of the problems of literary criticism of seventeenth-century German poetry has been perhaps the failure to distinguish such explanation and clarification from interpretation. More exactly, it has been the tendency in dealing with a poem to stop after the former, leaving the implication for the reader either that the poem in question needs no interpretation or that such clarification and explanation *is* in fact an interpretation. A case in point is the above-mentioned application of *Geistesgeschichte* to poetry. Similar distortion occurs when elements of an individual poem are related to and explained by reference to theories of poetics current at the time the poem was written. In each case the movement is away from the poem, the appeal to some other law than that of the work itself. The method too often involves forcing a given poem to fit certain general pre-

---

ed. Egon Schwarz, Hunter G. Hannum, and Edgar Lohner (Göttingen, 1967), pp. 9–28.

scriptions or laws which are assumed valid for all and which exist outside the universe of the poem. To the extent that any such prescription is presented as the regulating norm for an entire period of literature in so formidable a fashion that the literary critic sees no need to assume or simply does not bother to notice the possible deviations from that norm in the individual example, to this extent the generalization has become self-sufficient and of primary significance, and the prospects for viewing a single poem as a single poem grow slimmer.

The following studies are a frank combination of explanation and interpretation. An honest attempt has been made to distinguish between the two in such a way as to have the former serve the latter. As such, the essays are based on the belief that, despite the extraliterary pressures of what we artificially and at times arbitrarily choose to call a period of literature, the individual creative ego cannot be denied as master of its creation even in the most normative of ages. Literary critics and literary historians, without failing to realize the force of tradition, indeed necessarily considering fully its various aspects, must, nevertheless, not fail to recognize a poem as the basically individual and coherent entity it is.

# 2

## Es ist alles eitell

Gerhard Fricke maintains that much of the weakness of Gryphius' images stems from too great an adherence to seventeenth-century poetic principles and the rules of rhetoric contained therein—to a method which bases the choice of a particular image not on any fundamental organic connection between it and the concept or object it is to represent, but on its being merely externally and rather superficially an apt phrase. In indicating the lack of individuality in newly created compound words, he emphasizes that any one word could be replaced, at the whim of the poet, by an abundance of other possibilities, just as it in turn might as easily serve as a decorative metaphor for a whole series of possibly quite unrelated objects. He cites the well-known section from *Das Buch von der deutschen Poeterei* where Opitz offers, by way of example, as suitable metaphors for either night *or* music the new formations *Arbeitttrösterin* and *Kümmerwenderin,* just as "das gleich darauf genannte Compositum 'Wolkentreiber' nicht nur für den 'Nortwind,' sondern auch für jeden anderen verwendbar wäre" ("the compound listed directly thereafter, 'Wolkentreiber,' could be applied not only to the north wind, but also to any other wind").[1] For

1. *Die Bildlichkeit,* p. 14.

this reason, according to Fricke, this basic lack of identity between the word and the object to which it refers, which is in turn caused by the absence of the binding force of subjectivity, Gryphius' images can yield only the parallelism of allegory and never attain the unity of true symbol. The ultimate result of such practice is the loss of meaning of even the seemingly most concrete of expressions.[2] And yet, despite Fricke's argument, which is generally convincing, there is a starkness and earnestness about much of Gryphius' poetry which prevents the imagery from becoming merely decorative and functionless. Its ambiguity often heightens, rather than lessens, its effectiveness and makes it difficult to picture Gryphius as the detached and mechanical poem-producer that he has frequently been made out to be. It is this haziness about many of the images, a hovering, it seems, between two or more levels of meaning, combined with a strikingly sensitive use of sound, rhythm, and form, which contributes greatly to the beauty of much of his poetry.

" 'Was hätten wir erwarten dürfen, wenn Gryphius nicht so früh gestorben wäre!' fragt Palm. Variationen über das Thema *Vanitas vanitatum vanitas* läutet die Antwort wenigstens für den Lyriker Gryphius." ( " 'What could we have expected if Gryphius had not died so young!' asks Palm. Variations on the theme of *Vanitas vanitatum vanitas* is the answer, at least for Gryphius the lyric poet.")[3] Thus speaks Victor Manheimer on the subject of Gryphius' lyric poetry, and it cannot be denied that probably in no other major poet of seventeenth-century Germany do the themes of time, transience, and death occur with such compulsive insistence and almost pathological concentration. They very likely also reach an artistic peak in his sonnets and odes. So it is fitting that we begin with one of the most famous of his poems on this theme, one which has also been the object of repeated study and analysis. Much of the discussion of this sonnet has centered on the textual differences between the original version, number six in the *Lissaer Sonettbuch* of 1637, and the revision of 1643, which was prepared by the author for the new Leyden edition of his poetry. Of the two versions, which follow, the second is the usually accepted one and is printed in most current and earlier anthologies:

2. *Die Bildlichkeit*, pp. 174–75, 220–34.
3. Victor Manheimer, *Die Lyrik des Andreas Gryphius* (Berlin, 1904), p. 195.

## VANITAS, VANITATUM, ET OMNIA VANITAS

Es ist alles gätz eytel. Eccl. I. v. 2
(All is vanity. Eccles. 1: 2)

Ich seh' wohin ich seh / nur Eitelkeit auff Erden /
    Was dieser heute bawt / reist jener morgen ein /
    Wo jtzt die Städte stehn so herrlich / hoch vnd fein /
Da wird in kurtzem gehn ein Hirt mit seinen Herden:
Was jtzt so prächtig blüht / wird bald zutretten werden:
    Der jtzt so pocht vnd trotzt / läst vbrig Asch vnd Bein /
    Nichts ist / daß auff der Welt könt vnvergänglich seyn /
Jtzt scheint des Glückes Sonn / bald donnerts mit beschwerden.
    Der Thaten Herrligkeit muß wie ein Traum vergehn:
    Solt denn die Wasserblaß / der leichte Mensch bestehn
Ach! was ist alles diß / was wir vor köstlich achten!
    Alß schlechte Nichtigkeit? als hew / staub / asch vnnd wind?
    Als eine Wiesenblum / die man nicht widerfind.
Noch wil / was ewig ist / kein einig Mensch betrachten!
                                            (*Werke* 1: 7)

(I see wherever I turn only vanity on earth.
What one man builds today, another tears down tomorrow,
Where now proud cities stand, majestic, high, and fine,
There ere long will walk a shepherd with his herds:
What blooms so lovely now will soon be trampled down:
Who boasts now and defies, will leave mere dust and ashes,
Nothing in this world could ever be eternal.
If Fortune's sun shines now, she'll thunder soon with hardships.
The splendor of our deeds must pass away like dreams:
Can, then, this frail soap bubble, fragile man, remain?
Oh! what is everything that we consider precious,
But wretched emptiness, but dry weeds, dust, ash, and air?
But a wild flower on the meadow which one will find no more.
And yet, no one will contemplate what lies beyond all time.)

### Es ist alles eitell

Du sihst / wohin du sihst nur eitelkeit auff erden.
    Was dieser heute bawt / reist jener morgen ein:
    Wo itzund städte stehn / wird eine wiesen sein
Auff der ein schäffers kind wird spilen mitt den heerden.
Was itzund prächtig blüht sol bald zutretten werden.

Was itzt so pocht undt trotzt ist morgen asch vnd bein.
Nichts ist das ewig sey / kein ertz kein marmorstein.
Itzt lacht das gluck vns an / bald donnern die beschwerden.
Der hohen thaten ruhm mus wie ein traum vergehn.
Soll den das spiell der zeitt / der leichte mensch bestehn.
Ach! was ist alles dis was wir für köstlich achten /
Als schlechte nichtikeitt / als schaten staub vnd windt.
Als eine wiesen blum / die man nicht wiederfindt.
Noch wil was ewig ist kein einig mensch betrachten.
(*Werke* 1: 33)

(You see wherever you turn only vanity on earth.
What one man builds today, another tears down tomorrow:
Where now proud cities stand will be a meadow soon,
On which a shepherd's child will dally with his herds.
What blooms so lovely now will soon be trampled down.
What boasts now and defies will be tomorrow's dust and ashes.
Nothing is that is eternal, neither bronze nor marble
                                        [monument.
If Fortune now smiles on us, she'll thunder soon with hardships.
The fame of splendid deeds must pass away like dreams.
Can then Time's hapless plaything, fragile man, remain?
Oh! what is everything that we consider precious,
But wretched emptiness, but shadow, dust, and air?
But a wild flower on the meadow which one will find no more.
And yet, no one will contemplate what lies beyond all time.)

Whether or not one agrees with Joseph Leighton's verdict in a brief article devoted to the revision of a single line of this sonnet, it must be said that his comments raise far-reaching implications. For Leighton argues that the changes in line seven are not dictated solely by a mere striving for closer adherence to Opitzian theory and thus by an unusual degree of concern for the superficialities of external form and poetic nicety, the result of which is detrimental to the poem as a whole; rather, he sees in the revision a more subtle awareness, on the part of Gryphius, of the unity and inner structure of his sonnet than is usually credited to the poet.[4] By thus differing with the prevailing analyses of this poem and by seeking to sub-stantiate his views by evidence of an internal unity of composition, Leighton necessarily questions a significant aspect of what has threatened to become the accepted posture in the critical evalua-

4. "On the Interpretation of Andreas Gryphius's Sonnet 'Es ist alles eitell,'" *MLR* 60 (1965): 225–28.

tion of Gryphius' poetry. While both his well-taken point in line seven and his method of arriving at his conclusions are worthy of support, it is not possible to agree with his concession that the best-known recent commentators of this poem, Marian Szyrocki and H. G. Haile, are otherwise correct in claiming that Gryphius generally weakened the imagery elsewhere by revisions which brought no gain to the sonnet. Nor is there the need to seek justification for a further interpretation of this sonnet, which, I am afraid, must take the form of more than the "mild protest" that Leighton suggests, for, as he himself notes, the analyses of "Es ist alles eitell" have thus far failed to do justice to the poet—or to the poem. Leighton has made a good start, but he does not go far enough. Any attempt to consider the other changes in the poem which Leighton does not treat must deal with these earlier interpretations, in which an unsettling process of critical calcification of a sort seems to have taken place. These, in turn, have resulted to some extent from more general judgments on the nature of Gryphius' lyric.

The influence of Manheimer's extraordinary emphasis on the unoriginal and the impersonal, on the stylized and normative features of the poetry, has already been alluded to in the introduction. On the question of revisions in general, Manheimer concedes that there may be more than one reason for any single change that a poet decides to make. Significantly, however, despite this concession, where Gryphius is concerned his contention is firm that the revisions most often represent simply a bowing to convention, in whose net an older poet is inextricably bound. No longer possessed of the need to speak out directly or of the passion to do so, as was the youth, the older poet-critic, in reviewing his early poems, finds his task to be the removal of the subjective and the substitution of an impersonal tone. It is, really, a process of correction, rather than revision, which Gryphius, at least, undertakes "als Mensch des 17. Jahrhunderts nach Rezepten, die beispielsweise auch Opitz kannte" ("as a man of the seventeenth century, according to prescriptions which, for instance, were known to Opitz, too"). Nowhere, in fact, does he cite a change which was made for reasons that are significantly different or one which results in the actual improvement of a poem as an artistic whole. For that matter, we are led to believe that Gryphius himself, as a child of his age, was not in the least concerned with reshaping his poetry for this purpose: "Es ist ihm niemals um die Vertiefung, überhaupt um den Gang oder die

Nuancierung seiner Gedanken, um das Gefüge und die Verbind-
ungen in einem Gedicht als *Ganzem* zu tun; als Sohn seiner Zeit
ist ihm, solange er wenigstens nur umarbeitet, die Ahnung einer
inneren Form stets fern geblieben. Er hält sich an einzelnes, geht
von Vers zu Vers, höchstens einmal von einer Versperiode zur
nächsten; er 'dichtet' also nicht eigentlich um, wie man das von den
Dichtern des 19. Jahrhunderts sagen kann, sondern er bleibt im
Korrigieren stecken." ("He is never concerned with the depth, with
the continuity or the nuances of his thoughts at all, or with the
structure and the unifying elements in a poem as a *whole*; as a
child of his age, at least so long as he is merely rewriting, the concept of inner form always remained far from his mind. He works on
individual elements, moves from verse to verse, at the most, occasionally, from one unit of verse thought to the next; thus he does
not really 'revise,' as can be said of the poets of the nineteenth
century. Rather, he remains at the level of correcting.")[5]

Szyrocki, who at times displays a disconcerting inclination to
restate Manheimer's opinions, concurs fully on such matters and
runs the risk of confusing poet with poem. Charging that the variations introduced in the second version of the Lissa sonnets followed
from Gryphius' dependence on and conscious acceptance of various
stylistic conventions, conformity to which, in turn, caused increased

---

5. Manheimer, p. 67. Cf. also p. 101: "Wenn ein Dichter, älter und
kühler geworden, seine Gedichte, die vielleicht einer jungen und warmen
Stunde entströmt waren, als Kritiker wiedervornimmt und durchkorrigiert, dann
steht er als der technisch erfahrene und gereifte Vertreter einer *Konvention*
(wenn auch nur seiner eigenen) den vielleicht stammelnden, aber doch mehr
oder weniger elementar und grade so erlebten Produkten seiner Schöpfer-
kraft gegenüber. Vielleicht hatte er als *Jüngling* das Bedürfnis sich mitzuteilen,
von sich zu sprechen; die Konvention dringt auf Unpersönlichkeit, und der
*Mann* tilgt vorsichtig, was ihm jetzt zu subjektiv erscheint. Die gesellschaft-
liche, die literarische, die religiöse Konvention, in denen er steht, pflegen so
mächtig zu sein, daß sie ihm Änderungen nahelegen, die mit sprachlich-
künstlerischen Motiven wenig Berührung haben." ("When a poet, who has
become older and less emotional, takes up again his poems, which poured
forth originally perhaps from some youthful and passionate moment, and reads
them through again as a critic, then he confronts these products of his creative
power, which were originally uttered perhaps in stammering words, but were
nonetheless the products of elemental experiences, as the technically seasoned
and mature representative of a *convention* (even if it be only his own). Perhaps as a *youth* he had a need to communicate, to speak of himself; convention demands the impersonal, and the *man* cautiously revises away what seems
to him now to be too subjective. The social, literary, religious conventions in
which he stands tend to become so powerful that they force upon him revisions
which have little to do with matters of language or art.")

objectivity and the wholesale purging of the personal, *das Erlebte,* he concludes in a specific reference to this collection of poems: "Nach Jahren, als der Dichter in den Niederlanden eine Neuausgabe plante, arbeitete er die Sonette um. In der vorgenommenen Verbesserung versuchte Gryphius, den neuen Sprachanforderungen der Zeitgenossen im Sinne der Korrektheit gerecht zu werden, um nicht dem Verdacht der Ungelehrtheit ausgesetzt zu sein. Die Tatsache aber, daß er die Verbesserungen sozusagen als Massenarbeit 'am Schreibtisch, zeitlich entfernt von dem Erlebnis des Schaffensprozesses,' vornahm, so wie der Einfluß des Zeitstils zogen eine Steigerung der Objektivität nach sich bei gleichzeitiger Entrückung des Persönlichen und Erlebten." ("Years later, when the poet was planning a new edition in the Netherlands, he revised the sonnets. In the revisions which he undertook, Gryphius attempted to satisfy the linguistic requirements of his contemporaries in the sense of correctness, in order not to leave himself vulnerable to the suspicion of being unlearned. However, the fact that he undertook the revisions wholesale, so to speak, 'sitting at his desk, removed in time from the experience of the creative process,' as well as the influence on him of the current style of writing, caused an increase in objectivity with a simultaneous removal of what was personal and directly experienced.")[6]

H. G. Haile, in one of the most recent articles on "Es ist alles eitell," arrives at a similar conclusion regarding that poem specifically: "The representative formula has triumphed in the revision, and we have lost the poet behind his words."[7] But, through careful reading of the two versions without preconceptions, it can be demonstrated that Gryphius' revisions cannot be so lightly relegated to the realm of solely mechanical correction, intentional or accidental "depersonalization," or the mere yielding—and out of fear for his reputation, at that—to prevailing stylistic formulas. Even if these assumptions were valid, however, such emphasis on experience, as though the first version of a poem could be equated with the emotional state of its author, is not clear. It would seem, indeed, that such remarks are themselves conditioned by a convention which demands that youthful spontaneity should be compared invidiously

6. *Der junge Gryphius,* Neue Beiträge zur Literaturwissenschaft, vol. 9 (Berlin, 1959), p. 95.
7. "The Original and Revised Versions of Two Early Sonnets by Andreas Gryphius: An Evaluation," *MLQ* 19 (1958): 312.

to mere correctness of a more advanced age. And if the revised version of this sonnet *could* be considered the "triumph of the representative," if it were so that we have "lost the poet behind his words," we would still have to ask: Does nothing more remain of the poem itself?

Stressing what he feels to be increased objectivity and movement away from the personal in the revisions, Manheimer offers as an example a tendency to avoid the first person by shifting to the second or the third in the rewritten poems, a consideration which has a direct bearing on the sonnet "Es ist alles eitell," the first in his list of those which contain this modification. According to Szyrocki, the change in person in line one from "Ich" to "Du" must be laid to sheer chance, since the poet was actually concerned with removing the two instances of apocope in the original "seh'."[8] He does not dwell on the matter, pointing out only that by choosing "Du sihst" as a substitute, Gryphius was able to come closest, under the circumstances, to the content and style of the 1637 sonnet. The change in person is central to Haile's interpretation, however. After quoting the Manheimer comments cited above for general support on the avoidance of "Ich," Haile continues: "The first word of the sonnet, 'Du,' represents no minor change. It alone literally reverses our whole point of view. It is obvious that the use of the second person forces greater distance between audience and poet, who may even seem to assume the role of preacher."[9] The statement is not convincing, however. Neither the "greater distance between audience and poet" nor the reversal of "our whole point of view" is at all obvious—except only "literally," if "Ich" and "Du" are taken in a contextual vacuum, as in a textbook paradigm; there, following only the letter of the laws of grammar and language structure, if one accepts the two words as simply pronouns born of the linguistic necessity of distinguishing between a person speaking and one spoken to, the separation between them is clear. But this is a poem,

8. Szyrocki, pp. 95 ff. Manheimer, speaking of a general tendency toward elimination of apocope in Gryphius' revisions, points out also that there are, nevertheless, exceptions, especially in rhyming syllables, the imperative, and occasionally at the caesura. This, together with the fact that, curiously, from around 1650 Gryphius not only did not pay so much attention to the removal of apocope, but that, on the contrary, new instances appeared and in some cases old ones which had once been revised away reappeared in a third version, makes the excessive emphasis on such corrections as a cause of revision at least open to question.

9. "The Original and Revised Versions of Two Early Sonnets," p. 312.

not a grammar book. Haile's claim goes unsupported, except for the quotation from Manheimer, whose own broad generalizations on these matters are by no means proven by the enumeration of similar changes from the first person in other poems, especially since he refuses to consider alternative reasons for this revision, wherever it occurs. Certainly the contention that, in itself, the shift from "Ich" to "Du" causes so radical a change in the tone of the whole sonnet, such a heightened depersonalization and increased distance between poet and reader, is not valid. Indeed, if behind this revision had lain such a fear of the subjective, one cannot but wonder why Gryphius did not turn to the obvious—the clearly impersonal "man siht," which would have served his purpose neatly, at the same time avoiding the apocope and lending that degree of elevated distance suitable for his stance as "preacher."[10]

Nor is the argument that places the poet in the role of preacher borne out either by the tone of this sonnet or by the appearance of a similar posture elsewhere in Gryphius' poetry. Although such a role is only hinted at first, it is necessary for Haile's thesis, and he returns to the point with more certainty. In drawing his main conclusions about the poem, he maintains that by assuming the preacher's role and creating that distance by the change in person, Gryphius finally excludes himself from the guilt of vanity which he had accepted personally before: "If it is 'du' who bears the guilt declared by line 14, then the heart has gone out of the sonnet. In N,* one human who would not consider "was ewig ist" was he who had confessed, 'Ich seh' wohin ich seh' / nur Eitelkeit auff Erden.' He had described the vain, attractive world, had repeated, 'Nichts ist . . . auff der Welt.' When at last he used the word 'ewig,' it was to lament the spiritual vanity of mankind, himself included. This was the force of the *pointe*, undermined in B.* Here, the vital preparation in line 7 is destroyed; but most damaging to the *pointe* is the disappearance behind ecclesiastical 'du' of guilty 'ich.' "[11] The vital preparation in line seven for the undermined *pointe* in B of

10. Only recently, Karl Otto Conrady, in his excellent study, *Lateinische Dichtungstradition und deutsche Lyrik des 17. Jahrhunderts,* Bonner Arbeiten zur deutschen Literatur, vol. 4 (Bonn, 1962), has questioned this methodology, with specific, though brief, reference to the shifts from "Ich" to "Du" in Gryphius' revisions (p. 230).

11. "The Original and Revised Versions of Two Early Sonnets," p. 314 (Asterisks: N refers to the 1637 version of the Lissa book of sonnets, B to the 1643 version).

which Haile here speaks is the qualification that nothing "auff der Welt" is lasting, which he considers to have the effect of allowing the possibility for permanence somewhere else—a "somewhere else" which becomes explicit only in the last line. It is perhaps too obvious to point out that the same qualification appears in line one and is not revised away. But more important at this point is the fact that "Du" of the revision seems clearly to have a self-inclusive, generalizing function—not "you others"—and that the poet, or speaker, himself is still a member of the group. Thus there is no reason to assume, from the poem itself, any fear of the "too personal" as the cause, or increased objectivity and distance as the result, of the shift. Nor, then, need we suppose that Gryphius excludes himself from the guilty in line fourteen: "Noch wil was ewig ist kein einig mensch betrachten."

Why, then, the revision? We do not need to consider the sound patterns of the poem in detail to notice the definite recurrence of certain vowel sounds in the revised version. It is strange indeed that no critic has seen fit to mention the appearance of *ie* and *u*, the vowels of the central image "wiesen blum," in the significant revisions of lines three, four, nine, and ten. That the sounds of the revised "Du sihst," stressed all the more by repetition in line one, fit perfectly into this harmony, cannot be denied. Nor can there be a doubt about the thematic relationship between virtually all of the images containing these sounds—thus "wiesen" and "blüht" of lines three and five are echoed in "wiesen blum" of thirteen, while "spilen" of line four is mirrored by "spiell der zeitt" of line ten. At the same time, this repetition supports a more extensive vowel pattern which develops fully only in the revised sonnet. Already present but in unobtrusive isolation in the original line two, the contrast of the front and back vowels *i* and *ei* is clearly strengthened by the combination of revisions in lines one (*"sihst . . . sihst . . . eitelkeit"*), three (*"wiesen* sein"), four (*"spilen"*), seven (*"sey / kein . . . kein marmorstein"*), and ten (*"spiell der zeitt . . . leichte"*). The pertinent revisions in these lines are italicized. Nor is this the only evidence that the poet's sensitive ear played a major role in the revisions which have been so lightly attributed to the force of convention. The echoing play of vowels and vowel and consonant combinations in lines six through nine is brought about largely by the changes Gryphius chose to make in these lines. Especially noteworthy in the new version are such subtle and effective sound recapitulations as "morgen asch vnd bein . . . kein ertz kein marmorstein" in six and seven, and "thaten ruhm . . . traum" in nine. Even seemingly minor revisions, such as that from "donnerts mit" to "donnern die beschwerden" in line eight and the new "schaten" of line twelve (in its proximity to the rhyming "achten" and "betrachten" of lines eleven and fourteen) are apparently based on sound. Gryphius was certainly not unaware of the poetic function of created sound patterns. Such striking repetition, contrast, and interweaving of sounds, occurring so often precisely at the points of revision in this sonnet, can hardly be laid to chance. The resulting harmony, whether the product of the poet's conscious consideration or of his unconscious feeling for the role of sound in lyric poetry, binds and emphasizes much of the imagery and generally works as a unifying force in the poem.

But the value and function of the new images inserted in these lines, the poet's intent, and the results obtained must also be weighed. In Szyrocki's opinion, Gryphius rewrote lines three and four to avoid the caesura rhyming of "stehn" and "gehn" of the original. He condemns further the artificiality of the new image in line four—"Auff der ein schäffers kind wird spilen mitt den heerden"— which he terms "wiederum ein Zugeständnis Gryphius' zugunsten des Zeitstils" ("one more instance of Gryphius' yielding to the pressures of current stylistic prescription").[12] Although more specific, Haile is no less critical: "Inclination towards the representative formula may, to our taste, render pleasing simplicity sweet and cloying, as in line 4 ('schäferskind,' 'spielen'); but the reviser's style demands the representative."[13] I fail to see the significantly more positive features of the first version and the more negative qualities of the second when the two images are compared. But the changes are more complex, and the ideas of a great poet cannot be so handily disposed of without a closer examination of the effect of these changes on the sonnet as a whole. Erich Trunz, in what is probably the most perceptive and generally successful interpretation of this poem, has seen something of the beauty and complexity of the images in lines three, four, and thirteen, but does not grasp their full significance. Trunz correctly points out the twofold nature of the new images in lines three and four; on the one hand, he notes a hint of the idyllic, on the other, the clear implication of the de-

12. Szyrocki, p. 98.
13. "The Original and Revised Versions of Two Early Sonnets," p. 313.

struction of that which is created by man.[14] In reworking the two
lines, Gryphius lends support to that idyllic quality by drastically
changing the sound. He removes the harsher stops and velars and
replaces them with more softly flowing sibilants and labials, at the
same time creating an assonance and alliteration which link the
three main components of idyllic innocence in the scene: "schäffers
kind," "spilen," and "wiesen." Trunz comments that the antitheses
so carefully drawn in the second and third lines temporarily disappear in line four. This is true metrically and rhythmically, but only
apparently so in the imagery. For, although the new image re-
placing "Hirt" in that line does help to underscore that already
mentioned impression of innocence and peace, there is an ambiguity about the new line which, at the same time, yields a sense
of powerlessness and purposelessness, a hint of that helplessness of
man which is, after all, the theme of the sonnet. There is no longer
serious work being done by man, no leading of the flock by a trusted
shepherd, but a mere playing of children.

Szyrocki feels that "spiell der zeitt" replaced "Wasserblaß" in
line ten because of "Betonungsschwierigkeiten." Haile, to whom
the new image is merely a cliché, cites and accepts Manheimer's
argument that Gryphius removed the "stronger" original "for the
sake of propriety." One wonders whether in fact "Wasserblaß" was
any less a formula than its replacement, and whether Gryphius can
again be charged with revising out of fear of giving offense. If
Haile is correct in asserting that the word had a "disagreeable connotation" (Manheimer's *"trivialen Nebensinn"*) which would affect
the reader so strongly that Gryphius chose to delete it, we should
expect to find that other writers also avoided it. But the article in
Grimm's *Wörterbuch* reveals extensive use of this popular word
from the fifteenth to the eighteenth century, both in the expected
meaning of *Seifenblase* and, as a metaphor to express the frailty
of man, with apparently no fear of possible misunderstanding because of the connotation alluded to by Haile and Manheimer.
Whatever one's opinion about the quality of this new image, it can
hardly be said, from the evidence presented, that the poet was here
concerned solely with the individual word and made the change
for reasons of propriety. It is equally clear that the revisions in
lines three, four, and ten were not undertaken merely because

14. "Es ist alles eitel," in *Die deutsche Lyrik*, ed. Benno von Wiese,
vol. 1 (Düsseldorf, 1959), 146 ff.

"such turns of speech were standard, representative, and hence preferable formulations."[15] I have already discussed the patterns of sound and echo created by them in these lines. That, in addition, "spiell der zeitt" and the new image of line four complement each other conceptually indicates far more than an urge for correctness on Gryphius' part. Man, whose actions and fate are determined by apparently blind and uncaring external forces which he cannot comprehend, tyrannically ruled by, hopelessly bound to, and mercilessly toyed with by time, can only really play at life, much as the shepherd's child in line four.

Haile offers as a possible reason for the change in line nine from "Der Thaten Herrligkeit" to "Der hohen thaten ruhm" the desire to avoid too great an affirmation of and display of attachment to a life supposedly *eitel*. The word "herrlich" has also disappeared from line three, he notes. The argument, in itself weak, does not gain from the fact that the equally affirmative "prächtig" remains in the revised line five. Had the poet been so concerned, we assume he would also have been consistent. Nor is it clear why the original expression is less a cliché than the new one, as Haile here insists. On the other hand, something can be said for the revision if, again, the poem is considered as an artistic whole. "Der Thaten Herrligkeit," referring possibly to material achievements, does not adequately or clearly express Gryphius' intent. At this point in the sonnet, the poet has already devoted the greater part of eight lines to the vanity of the material trappings of life. Now in its climax, he is ready to declare the insubstantiality of proud man himself. He cannot argue, however, that since material things must pass away, so, obviously, must man. This one creature stands at the peak of creation. In value and importance he towers above his buildings, his cities, and, indeed, the natural world about him. Gryphius needs something unquestionably higher, something whose supreme worth is universally recognized, against which to measure man in order to make properly clear his fragility. How better stress man's real lack of substance than to emphasize that even immaterial fame, which cannot be similarly subject to corrosion and decay, nevertheless, "mus wie ein traum vergehn"? The humanistic ideal of the immortality of the poet's reputation had by no means been completely displaced in the seventeenth century. Only three years before the revision of this sonnet, Paul Fleming, on his deathbed,

15. "The Original and Revised Versions of Two Early Sonnets," p. 313.

could find consolation in a reputation that would live after him:
"Man wird mich nennen hören, / Biß daß die letzte Glut diß Alles
wird verstören." ("My name will still be celebrated, / Until that
final fire will cause all things to vanish.")[16] Furthermore, in view of
the evident care which Gryphius takes with the sound of his lines,
we cannot overlook the new resonance of lines eight and nine taken
together in the 1643 version. The back vowels *a, o, u,* and *au* are
now heavily represented, producing a deep, somewhat-muted un-
dertone, a rumbling murmur that extends throughout the length of
each line. With the elimination of the *ei* from the first half of each
line, the sharper contrasts between line halves that existed before
have disappeared. The sounds, allowed now to rebound from and
echo one another, reverberate with a new fullness. In line eight,
for example, even the unaccented *e*'s have been replaced in the
first half by an echoing *a* and *u,* and the new sequence of long *o, a,*
and *u* in the first three stressed syllables of line nine effectively
picks up the sounds of line eight once again.

In connection with the revisions, one final matter remains. It
is, of course, possible that Haile's assumption about the change in
line three (from "Wo jtzt die Städte stehn so herrlich / hoch vnd
fein" to "Wo itzund städte stehn / wird eine wiesen sein") is correct—that is, that in the 1637 sonnet the young poet's own emotions
were strong enough to break through the rigidity of standard rhetorical formula. It would probably indicate, in Haile's terms, the
momentary triumph of the individual over the representative, a
supposition which nicely supports his interpretations of the two
poems. But we must ask, what do poet and poem lose by the revision? What did they gain in the original? As descriptive adjec-
tives signifying nothing but general approval, "herrlich," "hoch,"
and "fein" seem no less clichés than "spiell der zeitt" and "schaten,"
which Haile lists as such. He observes that in the original sonnet
there is a break in tone at the caesura of line three—but once
again the question is, how does this help the poem? Haile views
the change as yet another instance of Gryphius' yielding to rhetoric
and formula. Adherence to poetic formula, he claims, which en-
courages pronounced contrast, leads to the balancing of "städte"
with "wiesen."

16. *Paul Flemings deutsche Gedichte,* ed. J. M. Lappenberg, vol. 1, p.
460, in Bibliothek des literarischen Vereins in Stuttgart, vol. 82 (Darmstadt,
1865).

Whatever the reason for the revision in line three, I must question whether the result is really a weakening of the sonnet. Aside from the imagery introduced, the rhythmic pattern of antithetical half-lines begun in line two is, of course, strengthened. This pattern, paralleled in lines five, six, and eight, persists, despite the interruptions of four and seven, until the crushing force of lines nine and ten utterly destroys the positive side of the balance. The concern here seems to be form, rather than formula, and I suggest that, contrary to Manheimer's not very generous judgment, Gryphius is indeed concerned in these revisions with their effect on the poem as a whole rather than with isolated words. The tension created between an established pattern, thematic, rhythmic, or acoustic, and deviation from that pattern, when used by a sensitive and capable poet, comprises no small part of the very stuff of poetry. That the pattern here is consciously created and varied does not, in itself, detract from its poetic value or its effectiveness. By furthering, rather than muting, its development in the repetition of line three, Gryphius heightens all the more the intensity and finality of its ultimate destruction in lines nine and ten. In summary, the later version of this poem, far from being a weakening of the original, reveals rather a greater strength with respect to rhythmic sweep, as well as with respect to the unfolding of imagery and its thematic relevance.

As in so many of Gryphius' sonnets, the entire poem is directed toward, and finds completion of its meaning in, the one epigrammatic statement made in the last line, here a gentle *pointe*. Since the meaning is not fully realized until this line, there is a necessity of refocusing, of placing the first thirteen lines in proper perspective, and the reader must, in effect, review the entire sonnet from this vantage point. Line fourteen (and only line fourteen) takes up the precise rhythm of line one, thus referring the reader to it and confronting him for the first time explicitly with the central antithesis of the poem, the vanity of this earth and the eternal— the frame, both in concept and in form, in which the poem is enclosed. The last line of the sonnet cannot be regarded, as Trunz would have it, as a kind of afterthought or marginal note. Nor can it be said that the main "mood" of the poem is a sadness at the realization of the instability of man and his world. No strong emotional affirmation of the world is revealed in these lines. The wistful hint of peace and beauty, the evasive idyllic quality of the

images in lines three and four and of the wild flower in line thirteen
remain unclear and uncertain, and they function, after all, to emphasize rather than to diminish the essential thought of the perish-
ability of life. On the contrary, the main effect of line fourteen lies
in the very fact that it stands alone, this idea of eternity, in seeming insignificance against the unchecked forces of earthly decay.
And is not this at once the point of the poem, the apparent insignificance of the eternal to man? Its position at the end, so as to
offer the very last idea the reader takes from the sonnet, its rhythmic similarity to line one, and the fact that Gryphius does not here
turn to heavy rhetoric, but makes his point clearly and simply—all
this combines to make line fourteen stand out in relief, a case of
emphasis by understatement.

Although the references throughout the sonnet to the Book of
Ecclesiastes and the images borrowed from it are obvious, the tone
of the poetic word is not the same as that of the biblical word. If
Gryphius makes ample use of the language and phrasing of the
Scriptures, he does so, here as elsewhere, with no particular attention to the original context. Concerned as he is only with a confirmation of the insecurity and impermanence of human existence,
he selects those biblical images which give concise expression to
the one idea of transience. There is no elaboration of the themes.
As a result, he and the author of Ecclesiastes begin with similar
thoughts, but reach different conclusions and foster different overall
views of life. Aside from the idyllic overtones mentioned above,
which never become explicit, Gryphius' devaluation of all that is a
part of the earth is absolute. This negation is so complete that
even "the eternal" remains unnamed, mentioned in line seven only
in terms of what is *not* everlasting and in line fourteen by a description of man's negative reaction to it. By contrast, the author of
Ecclesiastes, despite the recognized fact of transience, always has
in mind a positive goal, a means of coming to terms with life and of
achieving whatever happiness is possible. Undaunted by its impermanence, he proceeds to set forth a set of rules for living. The
thoughts that everything on earth must pass "wie ein Schatten"
(8: 13), that life, determined by chance and time, is unstable and
unreliable (9: 11), that man's fate is to be forgotten by the world
after death (9: 5; 6: 4)—such reflections, all echoed in the Gryphius
sonnet, lead the author of the Scripture, nevertheless, to a fundamental resignation to and acceptance of life as it is through a final

affirmation of that which *is* of value in it. *Glück* and *Zeit* in Ecclesiastes are no less the inscrutable, inconsistent determinants of human activity, but, willfully toying with and actively attacking man, they can no longer be accepted by the poet Gryphius with the patience and dispassionate stoicism of unquestioning submission. If the antitheses of the sonnet never do exhibit that equilibrium so characteristic of the contrasts in the Book of Ecclesiastes, it is the complete and irrevocable collapse of a balance, at best tentative, in lines nine through twelve that sharply differentiates the poem from its "model." For Gryphius, one side of the scales is weighted too heavily. If the beauty of life emerges again momentarily in the "wiesen blum" of line thirteen, it can do so only timidly and tentatively, only not quite overwhelmed by its own fragility and frailty. There is no trace of the pulsing rhythm of life that lies at the heart of Ecclesiastes, that passionate recognition of the ineluctable, constant, and irreversible process of coming and passing away again. If the sonnet does conclude on a note of resignation, it is again of a different sort from that of the words of the Bible. For there is a perceptible sense of weariness about the manner in which the speaker of the poem, who does indeed seem to include himself with his "kein einig mensch," resigns himself—not to an acceptance of the inevitability of death and decay, but rather to a realization of the utter futility of being intellectually aware of facts so commonplace as to be unavoidable. Simply knowing the unchallengeable truth of the decay of the physical world does not result in man's turning from it and toward the spiritual world, which, he knows equally well, lies above and beyond it. And no amount of expressed disdain for the former can erase its existence or alter by one jot its fragile beauty, which, like the wildflower in the meadow, intrudes upon the mind and the senses, unbidden and with an insistence that cannot be stilled.

Clichés or not, the images "spiell der zeitt" and "wiesen blum" contain the essence of those concepts of time and of man as a plaything of time, of life as a game and an illusory deception, which are central to much of Gryphius' poetry. In order to illustrate the intensity with which Gryphius confronts these questions and expresses them in his poems, it would be helpful, before closing this chapter, to turn briefly to one of the more well-known odes which deals with themes similar to those that appear in the following sonnet:

Vanitas! Vanitatum Vanitas!

1. Die Herrlikeit der Erden
Mus rauch vndt aschen werden /
Kein fels / kein ärtz kan stehn.
Dis was vns kan ergetzen /
Was wir für ewig schätzen
Wirdt als ein leichter traum vergehn.

2. Was sindt doch alle sachen /
Die vns ein hertze machen /
Als schlechte nichtikeit?
Waß ist der Menschen leben /
Der immer vmb mus schweben /
Als eine phantasie der zeit.

3. Der ruhm nach dem wir trachten /
Den wir vnsterblich achten /
Ist nur ein falscher wahn.
So baldt der geist gewichen:
Und dieser mundt erblichen:
Fragt keiner / was man hier gethan.

4. Es hilfft kein weises wissen /
Wir werden hingerissen /
Ohn einen vnterscheidt /
Was nützt der schlösser menge /
Dem hie die welt zu enge /
Dem wird ein enges grab zu weitt.

5. Dis alles wirdt zerrinnen /
Was müh' vnd fleis gewinnen
Vndt sawrer schweis erwirbt:
Was Menschen hier besitzen /
Kan für den todt nicht nützen /
Dis alles stirbt vns / wen man stirbt.

6. Was sindt die kurtzen frewden /
Die stets / ach! leidt / vnd leiden /
Vnd hertzens angst beschwert.
Das süsse jubiliren /
Das hohe triumphiren
Wirdt oft in hohn vnd schmach verkehrt.

7. Du must vom ehren throne
Weill keine macht noch krone
Kan vnvergänglich sein.
Es mag vom Todten reyen /
Kein Scepter dich befreyen.
Kein purpur / gold / noch edler stein.

8. Wie eine Rose blühet /
Wen man die Sonne sihet /
Begrüssen diese Welt:
Die ehr der tag sich neiget /
Ehr sich der abendt zeiget /
Verwelckt / vnd vnversehns abfält.

9. So wachsen wir auff erden
Vnd dencken gros zu werden /
Vnd schmertz / vnd sorgenfrey.
Doch ehr wir zugenommen /
Vnd recht zur blütte kommen /
Bricht vns des todes sturm entzwey.

10. Wir rechnen jahr auff jahre /
In dessen wirdt die bahre
Vns für die thüre bracht:
Drauff müssen wir von hinnen /
Vnd ehr wir vns besinnen
Der erden sagen gutte nacht.

11. Weil vns die lust ergetzet:
Vnd stärcke freye schätzet;
Vnd jugend sicher macht /
Hatt vns der todt gefangen
Vnd jugend / stärck vnd prangen /
Vndt standt / vndt kunst / vndt gunst verlacht!

12. Wie viel sindt schon vergangen /
Wie viell lieb-reicher wangen /
Sindt diesen tag erblast?
Die lange räitung machten /
Vnd nicht einmahl bedachten /
Das ihn ihr recht so kurtz verfast.

13. Wach' auff mein Hertz vnd dencke;
Das dieser zeitt geschencke /

Sey kaum ein augenblick /
Was du zu vor genossen /
Ist als ein strom verschossen
Der keinmahl wider fält zu rück.

14. Verlache welt vnd ehre.
Furcht / hoffen / gunst vndt lehre /
Vndt fleuch den Herren an /
Der immer könig bleibet:
Den keine zeitt vertreibet:
Der einig ewig machen kan.

15. Woll dem der auff ihn trawet!
Er hatt recht fest gebawet /
Vndt ob er hier gleich fält:
Wirdt er doch dort bestehen
Vndt nimmermehr vergehen
Weil ihn die stärcke selbst erhält.

(*Werke* 2: 17)


(1. The splendor of this earth
Must turn to smoke and ashes,
No stone nor metal lasts.
The things that give us pleasure,
That we consider lasting,
Will pass away like fading dreams.

2. What are, then, all those things
Which serve to give us pleasure
But insubstantial frauds?
And what is human life,
Which drifts without foundation,
If not an image dreamed by time.

3. The glory we strive after,
And hold to be immortal,
Is merely false delusion.
When our last breath has left us,
And ruby lips have paled,
Then no one notes our deeds on earth.

4. Earthly knowledge aids us not,
From this vale we are torn

Regardless of our station.
What use enormous palaces?
He who finds the world too narrow
Will find his narrow grave too wide.

5. All this must soon dissolve
That costs such heavy toil,
That's won by the sweat of our brow.
Whatever we can here possess
Is after death so useless,
For all dies from us when we die.

6. What are our fleeting pleasures,
Never free from inner fears,
Burdened by constant sorrows.
Our sweetest jubilation,
Our greatest acts of triumph,
So often are transformed to shame and scorn.

7. You must yield the throne of honor,
For neither power nor crown
Can everlasting be.
No sceptre can release you,
Not gold, nor royal blood, nor precious stones,
From that final dance of death.

8. Just as the rose unfolds
When the early sun's first rays
Descend to greet the world,
But before the day declines
And the dusk of evening falls,
Wastes and falls without a warning,

9. So do we flower on earth,
And think to grow and flourish,
Of pain and worry free.
But ere we reach full growth
And come to our full blossom,
Our stems are snapped by death's gale winds.

10. We reckon year on year
And never see the bier
Placed right before our door.
And then we must take leave

Before we have the chance
To bid the world a last farewell.

11. While we enjoy our pleasures,
And strength seems limitless,
And youth appears to free us,
The chains of death imprison us,
And mock our strength and youth,
Our boasts, our rank, our skills, and favour.

12. How many are already dust,
How many blushing cheeks must
This day have already paled
Who planned a longer season
And did not even reason
That ours must be so short a stay.

13. Awake, my heart, consider
That all the gifts of time
Will linger but a moment.
What you enjoyed before
Has passed you like a current
That never will return again.

14. Deride the world and glory,
Fear, hope, gifts, and teachings,
And plead with Him for mercy
Who ever shall be King,
Whom time cannot drive out,
Whose power alone can make eternal.

15. Blessed be he who trusts in Him!
He has a strong foundation,
And though he may fall here,
There he will endure
And perish nevermore,
For the Power of Powers supports him.)

The ode seems very much like an expansion of the sonnet
"Es ist alles eitell," all of whose motifs are here repeated, enlarged
upon, and expressed in swiftly moving iambic verses of three or
four feet rather than in alexandrines. With its never-changing meter
and rhyme scheme, its constantly repeated idea, however varied

it may be in the individual strophes, the poem creates its own
monotony, both of structure and of content. For the most part,
there is no significant change in rhythm throughout, except for
the exclamations of the last three strophes. The result, at least for
the first seven stanzas, is a litany-like chant. Despite, or perhaps
because of, this monotony, the reader moves constantly forward.
Becoming accustomed to the unchanging rhythm and rhyme, he
begins to anticipate other structural patterns as well. A brief pause
at the rhyme word at the end of each line, for example, becomes
automatic, for most of the lines are so written that each contains a
syntactically complete segment of a thought. On the other hand,
no one line ever actually contains a complete thought, so that, despite the momentary pause, one moves forward steadily to the
conclusion of the poetic statement, which is finally reached in the
last line of each of the two three-line groupings that comprise every
stanza. In addition, there is a tension within the individual stanzas
which also causes the reader to anticipate and move forward. In
many cases, the second or third line of each group of three contains
a subordinate descriptive or interrupting element. Elsewhere, significant sentence elements which must be paired, such as subject
and verb, are separated by the line divisions. The reader attempts
to bridge as quickly and smoothly as possible the resulting gap between the beginning and the conclusion of a thought, and there are
no extraordinary syntactical or grammatical entanglements, no
problems of imagery or rhetoric, to impede his progress. This is
the prevailing pattern for the first seven stanzas.

In stanza eight, however, which is the exact center of this
fifteen-strophe ode, a sudden variation causes a short deviation
from the pattern and takes the reader by surprise. First, the clear
separation between the two sets of three lines each in the strophe,
which until now has been scrupulously maintained, vanishes; the
stanza does not divide into two complementary halves. Rather,
one thought continues for a full six lines. Furthermore, there can
be no pause at the end of line two, for the sense of the second and
third lines demands an enjambement which forces the reader immediately on to line three. By virtue of the apparent syntax of the
first two lines, the thought of the dependent clauses *could* end
with line two, but it does not. Should the reader pause here momentarily, as he has already become accustomed to doing in the
previous stanzas, he may well be deceived into reading "Begrüs-

sen" of line three as the verb of the main clause, the conclusion of the thought begun in line one. This is a pattern which he has seen before, for in the preceding stanzas the poet has frequently made such use of the first position in the line for the delayed verb of a main clause. Once the error has been made, the reader must return to the first line of the strophe and begin again in order to preserve the sense of the lines. But the deceptive quality of these verses goes even further. If "Begrüssen" should be read as the verb of the main clause, then "Die" of line four could at first reading be taken as its subject pronoun. Even if this is not the case, the referent of the relative "Die" is ambiguous. The pronoun may seem at first to refer to the closest grammatically possible noun, "diese Welt" of line three or, perhaps, "die Sonne" of line two. It refers to neither, but it is possible to read until the end of the strophe before the true antecedent becomes clear. Line six, with "Verwelckt" and "abfält," finally does make evident the connection between "Die" of line four and "eine Rose" of line one. Even now, however, although the antithesis upon which the stanza is structured is completed, the tension begun in line one with the subordinate "Wie" clause is not yet resolved, for the second half of the comparison comes only in stanza nine. The unifying main image of these two strophes, the blossoming and suddenly dying flower, which is so important also in the sonnet "Es ist alles eitell," has been stressed here both by its literally central position in the poem and by the exceptional structure of the stanzas in which it appears, with all their departures from what has come to be expected as the regular strophic pattern of the ode. In contrast to those that precede, stanzas eight and nine cannot be read through quickly; rather, because of structural difficulties that are unique in this poem, one must pause in the reading in order to connect the individual parts with one another and come from the lines with a coherent, whole thought, to which twelve verses rather than the usual three are devoted. Gryphius' theme is not simply that all things on earth inevitably pass away and thus are not to be valued, but that we react to them during our life as if they were in fact real and intrinsically valuable. It is the problem of *Sein/Schein,* and in strophes eight and nine of this ode, by means of an admirable poetic skill and sensitivity, the deception which is life and the world has become a deception on the level of language.

A complementary aspect of this theme is the speed with which the process of decay progresses, and stanza eight does in fact introduce a series of four stanzas all revolving about the idea of the swift passage of life. This rush of time leads to the poet's plea in strophes thirteen and fourteen—not to the Divine, but to himself— a plea which seems unnecessary after the insistent insights of stanzas one through twelve into the transitory character of all existence and the clarity of apparent acceptance with which they are expressed. But here again is that problem with which the speaker of our sonnet was forced to contend—after passively acknowledging the relative worthlessness of material existence, he finds himself yet faced with the necessity of convincing himself to turn actively toward Him "Der einig ewig machen kan" and the constancy of permanent existence in the realm of the eternal which He offers. It is certainly true that much of Gryphius' poetry, with its repeated and passionate condemnation of this world, seems to betray rather an underlying attachment to it and what must have proved a painful, continuous attempt to break free of it. One feels that it is not the reader, but the poet who must be convinced. Significantly, the eloquent talk in the ode of man's impermanence does not serve to emphasize the joys of eternal life or the glory of God. No characteristics of the Divine are given here, save that, in contrast to things of the earth, He is eternal. All that the poet seeks in eternity is permanence and rest, not so much from the material miseries of existence as from a life despotically controlled by time, with its unbearable arbitrary uncertainties and its lack of solid foundation, its deception, and its sudden changes. There is no plea for salvation, no talk of right or wrong, the righteous, or the sinful.

As is typical of Gryphius, verbs of intense motion dominate the ode. One by one the works of man are pronounced ephemeral and worthless, but the true horror of his position begins to appear only with strophe eight, with the direct confrontation of man by time and death, which attack him, ironically, when he should be at his strongest and seems most secure, and with the telescoping of time into its one significant aspect for man, the moment. Yet this is merely in keeping with the deception and illusion that is life. Man is born not to life, but into death, and he stands even as he matures in a one-sided battle with it. There is no peaceful process of growing old in Gryphius' poetry, for death is swift, violent, and unexpected. In his poems of this type, transience and death are such overwhelming forces that they appear to be the only meaningful characteristics of human life. Because of this inherent worthlessness and because man is deceived into nevertheless placing positive value on life, all human existence is *eitell*. Try as he may to be a positive active force, when seen in perspective against the tremendous forces of time which pursue him relentlessly from the moment of his birth, man is ultimately a passive absorber of the powers that work upon him. It is not so much the inevitability of death or actual physical suffering that torments him, but his necessary reliance upon an apparently fickle and uncaring higher power, a situation which results in the complete lack of any sort of firm foundation in life. There can be no agreement with the verse of Ecclesiastes: "Ein Jegliches hat seine Zeit, und alles Vornehmen unter dem Himmel hat seine Stunde"; there cannot be a time for living, and a time for dying, since, to Gryphius, man is dying from the moment of his birth. There does not, indeed, seem to *be* a time to live.

But death does hold out one promise—the chance to reach a final stopping place, the chance to leave the "racetrack" which is life. It is a place of rest, after all, for the exhausted traveler, who is perhaps best depicted by Gryphius in the sestet of the allegorical "Auf ein Jungfern-Spiel," which, after a deceptively frivolous octet, concludes with an extended cry of existential despair and disorder in a dreamlike race with neither goal nor competitors, nor even a clearly discernable pursuer:

> Seh ich Roxanen denn die Widrige nur an /
> Bald denck ich wie mit mir der Himmel spielen kan /
> Von dem ich minder noch weiß etwas zu erlangen /
> Ich wünsch / ich ruff / ich hoff / ich leid / ich streit / ich flieh /
> Ich irr / ich lauff / ich such / und finde nichts als Müh /
> Und daß mich alles jagt / und niemand doch wil fangen.
> (Werke 1: 126)

> (I need but to catch sight of the ugly maid Roxanne
> To realize full well how the Heavens can toy with me,
> Of whom I know still less how best to win their favor.
> I wish, I call, I hope, I suffer, fight, I flee,
> I search, I run, I lose my way, and gain nothing for my efforts,
> I only learn that all are chasing, but no one catches me.)

The lines are reminiscent of the political world of Gryphius' first drama *Leo Arminius,* where, as Klaus Günther Just aptly puts it, "jeder . . . Jäger und Gejagter zugleich ist" ("each person is at one and the same time hunter and prey").[17] It comes as no surprise when the poet comments in an earlier sonnet: "Diß Leben kömmt mir vor alß eine renne bahn" ("This life appears to me to be a running track").

17. "Andreas Gryphius und kein Ende?" *Schlesien* 10 (1965): 6–7.

# 3

## Auf die Geburt
## seines ältesten Sohnes Christiani

Willkommen süsses Kind / der Mutter höchste Lust /
  Doch die sich schier mit beyder Tod erkäufft /
  Willkommen Kind / das / weil die Nacht umläufft /
Mit neuer Freud erquickt des Vatern trübe Brust:
Wie? gleich um Mitternacht / ist dir denn nicht bewust
  Was Mitternacht / in der nur Furcht sich häufft:
  Und Wahn in Angst / und Angst in Weh sich täufft:
Wie? daß du denn gleich itzt das Leben grüssen must.
Diß ist der Engel Fest / die offt bey Nacht erschienen /
Die führen dich ins Licht / mit diesen solst du dienen /
  Dem / welcher dich aus Nacht hat in den Tag gebracht /
Die Engel kommen mit! O daß sie dich begleiten!
O daß sie durch die Welt / durch die gesetzten Zeiten /
  Dich führen wo ihr Heer um deinen Schöpffer wacht.
                    (*Werke* 1: 109)

(Welcome, my sweet child, your mother's greatest pleasure,
The price for which, it seemed at first, would be the death of
                                     [both.
Welcome, child, who, while night has us encircled,
Restores his father's saddened heart with new-found joy.
What? Born at the stroke of midnight? Can you not know

41

What meaning midnight holds? That time when fright
                                        [increases,
Delusion turns to fear, and fear leads on to woe?
Was there a need to greet the world precisely now?
This is the festival of angels, who oft by night appear.
They will lead you to the light, and with them you shall serve
Him, who once snatched us from night into the day.
The angels now approach! If only they go with you
And lead you through the world, through all created time,
To where the heavenly hosts surround and guard your Lord.)

Not even the traditionally joyful event of birth, indeed that of his
own eldest son, is spared the careful and skeptical scrutiny of
Gryphius, who can see none of man's joys as completely unmixed
blessings. Christian's birth is veiled in that same haze of ambiguity
and uncertainty that characterizes man's life on earth in so many
of Gryphius' poems. That the hour of his son's birth was literally
black serves only as a starting point from which the author can
proceed to demonstrate that life is surrounded by darkness of many
kinds. It has already been pointed out by Robert T. Clark, Jr., in
his interesting and penetrating article "Gryphius and the Night of
Time" that night has a peculiar and very personal meaning for the
poet.[1] Like the whole complex of words and images revolving
around the central concept of time, "Nacht" recurs again and again
in his poetry. In this sonnet it appears as that night in which man
is inevitably and inescapably rooted, a night which, however,
may lead to day. Above all, the moment of birth is man's link with
time, and in the short space of the sonnet Gryphius plays upon the
many possible connotations of night and time.

From the outset Christian is caught up of necessity in that
paradox of which life often seems to consist for his father, for the
image of life as projected by man appears to him to be only a distortion of its real nature. The very opening words of the sonnet,
"Willkommen süsses Kind," the greeting of the happy father, are
deceptive in their spontaneity and in the directness of their seemingly unqualified expression of happiness. With line two, however,
the blessing of a son's birth has already become ambiguous. It is an
ambiguity which is subtly reflected throughout the poem, not only

1. In *Wächter und Hüter. Festschrift für Hermann J. Weigand,* ed. Curt
von Faber du Faur, Konstantin Reichards, and Heinz Bluhm (New Haven,
1957), p. 65.

by its content, but also by Gryphius' use of rhyme and meter, the rhetorical devices of alliteration, assonance, and echo, but above all by the highly emotive uses of the word "Nacht" in its various meanings. These meanings, as they overlap and shift, help to create linguistically that very ambiguity and seeming paradox which characterizes man's life and which is the subject of this poem.

Line two stands in direct antithesis to line one—the welcome, despite the evident joy of the opening line, can be neither complete nor wholehearted, since Christian's first step into life, the actual moment of his birth, is closely linked with tragedy, the near-death of his mother. Paradoxically, man, at the very moment of his emergence into life, possesses unwillingly the power to destroy that which has created him, although it is a power over which he has no control. Even more, the newborn child itself nearly succumbs in the process of birth: "Doch die sich schier mit beyder Tod erkäufft." Although it may be truly the reflection of emotions deeply felt, the so-often-repeated antithesis joy/sorrow will by the end of the seventeenth century become, by too frequent exposure, a mere catchall phrase, a hackneyed expression which no longer *means*, but merely represents. While the antithesis sets the theme of this sonnet, in general terms, its meaning is also narrowed and deepened in verses one and two. Gryphius touches upon the central paradox of life in these lines, on the fundamental powerlessness of man in the face of the forces by which he is beset. In addition, there is already here a hint of the significance for Gryphius of the single moment in time, the "Augenblick." Not without cause nor accidentally is the moment so stressed in his poetry. Not only is man's death finally resolved in a single point of time (death coming in a moment after what often seems to Gryphius to have been the prolonged illness of life), but connected with it are paradoxes of intense interest to the poet. It is through the single moment that man reaches and becomes a part of the eternal:

Mein sind die Jahre nicht die mir die Zeit genommen /
Mein sind die Jahre nicht / die etwa möchten kommen
Der Augenblick ist mein / und nehm' ich den in acht
So ist der mein / der Jahr und Ewigkeit gemacht.
(*Werke* 2: 182)

(Mine are not the years that time has taken from me,
Mine are not the years that might perhaps yet follow.

The moment, that is mine, and if I choose to heed it,
Then He is mine who has created time and timelessness. )

The admonition of the epigram is not *carpe diem*; nor is its implication that by purposefully utilizing each moment of his life man
somehow becomes analogous to God the creator. Rather, the moment, any given moment, *may* become the means for the abolish-
ment of time and entrance into the *nunc stans*, the nondurational
eternal present. It would not do to dwell here on the possible influences on Gryphius of various religious philosophies or of the
types of mysticism which were in vogue in the seventeenth century. At least one similarity to these verses from Eastern religious
thinking is so striking, however, as to deserve brief mention: "The
instant, the present moment, the *nunc*, is called *ksana* in Sanskrit
and *khana* in Pali. It is by the *ksana*, by the 'moment,' that time is
measured. But this term has also the meaning of 'favourable moment,' 'opportunity,' and for the Buddhist it is by means of such a
'favourable moment' that one can escape from time. The Buddha
advises us 'not to lose the moment.' . . . He congratulates the monks
who 'have seized their moment' . . . and pities those 'for whom the
moment is past.' This means that after a long journey in cosmic time
. . . the illumination is instantaneous." And further, "Any instant
whatever, any *ksana* whatever, may become the 'favourable moment,' the paradoxical instant which suspends duration and throws
the Buddhist monk into the *nunc stans*, into an eternal present.
. . . The 'favourable moment' of enlightenment may be compared
with the flash that communicates a revelation, or with the mystical
ecstasy which is prolonged, paradoxically, beyond time."[2] In addition, Gryphius certainly senses in the moment the paradoxical fusion of time present and time past, a blurring of the dividing line
between becoming and passing away, as it is mirrored in the po-
tential fusion of birth and death in the moment of Christian's birth
above. This telescoping of time into a seeming simultaneity of
what has gone before and what is yet to come attaches with ma-
cabre significance to that transitory moment which is life itself. As
has been pointed out in the previous chapter, the awful irony of life
to Gryphius is that precisely when man should be at his strongest
and seems to be most secure—during his youth, the most marked

2. Mircea Eliade, *Images and Symbols. Studies in Religious Symbolism,*
trans. Philip Mairet (New York, n.d.), pp. 81 ff.

stage in the process of his becoming—he is, in the poet's eyes, already dying:

> Weil uns die lust ergetzet:
> Vnd stärcke freye schätzet;
> Vnd jugend sicher macht /
> Hatt vns der todt gefangen
> Vnd jugend / stärck vnd prangen /
> Vndt standt / vndt kunst / vndt gunst verlacht!

So it is that both past and future and man's attempts to control or regulate them by systematization, even on the most elementary level, are often viewed with irony, as in the sonnet "Auf den Anfang des 1660 zigsten Jahres" ("On the Beginning of the Year 1660"), in which the moment is likewise stressed:

> Wir zehlen was nicht ist und längst in nichts verschwunden /
>     Verwichner Zeiten Lauff und Menge vieler Jahr
>     Und was den Augenblick noch kaum verhanden war.
> Wir zehlen was sich noch nicht von der Zeit gefunden.
> Umsonst! wir Armen / Ach! Jahr / Monat / Tag und Stunden /
>     Sind kein beständig Gut / doch bringen sie Gefahr
>     Und höchsten Nutz zu uns. Sie bieten alles dar /
> Wordurch die Ewigkeit uns Menschen wird verbunden.
>     Gott dem nichts fällt noch kommt / dem alles steht und
>                                                 [blüht /
>     Der was noch künfftig ist als gegenwärtig sieht /
>     Wil auch vor Augenblick uns Ewigkeiten geben.
> Ach Seel! Ach! sey mit Ernst denn auf die Zeit bedacht/
> Nimm Jahr und Monat / Stund / und Augenblick in acht.
>     Ein einig Augenblick verspricht Todt oder Leben.
>                                         (*Werke* 1: 105)

> (We reckon what is not, and what has long since vanished,
> The course of faded times, the mass of many years,
> And what existed for us barely for a moment.
> We reckon what is not discovered yet by time.
> In vain, we wretched fools! Years, months, days, and hours,
> Are no one's lasting property, containing danger great,
> Yet advantageous to us. They represent those things
> By which eternity is bound to finite man.
> And God, who recognizes neither loss nor gain,

To whom the future is a never-changing present,
Will for a single moment eternity exchange.
Oh my soul! consider seriously what time can mean,
Take heed of years and months, of hours and every moment.
A single moment will deliver death or life.)

Both the structural antithesis and the conceptual paradox of the first two lines of the sonnet on the birth of Christian are continued throughout the first quatrain. Within the lines there is a kind of see-saw movement, a tugging back and forth between the two poles, which lends to them a distinctly dynamic quality. This becomes all the clearer if we try to crystallize the feelings expressed here of the father at the time of his son's birth. They remain ambiguous, revealing now the evident joy of the occasion, now the unexpected sorrow of which this moment yet becomes a part. The form of the lines supports their content, line one standing in antithesis to line two, line two to the first half of line three. If the beginning of line three with its greeting parallels and echoes the insuppressible happiness of line one, the jubilant cry of a rejoicing father is stilled once again with startling abruptness, interrupted rhythmically by the heavy pauses after the fourth and fifth syllables, and qualified by the sobering and strangely ominous thought of the second half of the line. We need not pause here to determine the precise meaning of "Nacht" in line three; it is enough that a connotation of gloom attaches to it. The second half of line three is in turn antithetically opposed to the first half of line four, and this latter again to the second half of line four. Significant, too, in this antithetical structure are the parallels and contrasts which develop between pairs of vowels. In line one the short *i, o,* and *u* and the modifications of the two latter vowels dominate in the expression of joyous welcome. This dominance is maintained until the middle of verse two; the second half of the line, however, is controlled by the sharply contrasting *ei, äu,* and long *o* sounds, which serve to introduce the darker, threatening element that attends Christian's birth. The first half of line three returns to the short *i/o* complex, which yields, in the ominous second half, to *ei* and *äu* once again. The play of vowels in line four, however, is more complex and makes the fact inescapable that sound and rhyme, by paralleling the sense, have an integral, functional role within the sonnet. The *eu* (*äu*) sound, which, within the pattern developed so far, has been used to express the threat of danger, and the *u*/*ü* sounds, which occur until now only in the context of joy, have been interchanged in the contrast "neuer Freud"/"trübe Brust," but remain antithetically juxtaposed. By making this shift, Gryphius is able to fashion the quartet in such a way that the rhyme phrases of lines one and four, "der Mutter höchste Lust"/"des Vatern trübe Brust," enclose the stanza in and focus attention on this central antithesis.

Within the first quartet the word "Nacht" appears for the first time. It is to occur in each of the four major segments of the sonnet at least once, except for the second tercet, where it is replaced by its partial synonym, "Zeiten." But the meaning of "Nacht" is unstable and complex, changing with each appearance in the poem. Although its negative connotations are apparent from the first, it must be examined anew for its precise meaning each time that it occurs, if, indeed, it is possible to speak at all of one clear meaning in any single instance. In line three, for example, "Weil die Nacht umläufft," "Nacht" certainly refers specifically to the particular night of Christian's birth, but it is equally clear that its meaning goes beyond this very concrete reference. Significant in this connection is Gryphius' choice of the verb "umläufft" rather than, perhaps, "umhüllt." With it, the poet goes metaphorically one step further—or, more correctly, he combines two steps in one. On the one hand, he depicts the envelopment of Christian's birth—and so of Christian himself—in literal darkness. At the same time and with the same image he proceeds away from the description of a static, sensorily perceived condition by adding that strikingly characteristic notion of time as it occurs throughout his works, time as an incessantly active, moving force. The entire emphasis here is on activity. With the use of the apparently intransitive verb, there is not even a recipient of the action, but only the action itself. Clearly negative from the context, this destructive metaphorical *Nacht* can only be the very period in which Gryphius himself lived, rife with all the fearful events of the Thirty Years' War, which was just now ending, and the devastation and misery left in its wake, the period into which he must now see his son born, too.

The gloomy "Mitternacht" is stressed both by its position in line five and by its repetition in line six. The general cloak of gloom that surrounds these lines is further strengthened by the parallelism of the rhetorical questions in lines five and eight and by the strong alliteration and assonance of line seven. While line eight maintains on the whole that darker side which is stressed throughout the quatrain, the tension begun in lines one through four is continued by the positive "grüssen," the incongruity of the friendly greeting of life amidst evidently inimical forces, and by the echo within this word of both "süsses" and "trübe." As if caught up in this constant fluctuation between joy and the presentiment of tragedy, "Nacht," too, wavers between a positive and a negative implication for man. Appearing in the second quartet as "Mitternacht," it is the symbol of the hostile supernatural forces that surround the birth, the hour of misfortune and fear in age-old superstitions. It may, of course, be quite true, as Gryphius states elsewhere, that both he and his oldest son were born at precisely this significant hour. If so, we can be certain that it seemed more than chance to the superstitious father. In "Mitternacht," then, is reflected once again that initial tension of the sonnet which first appears in lines one and two, midnight being traditionally the hour when the forces of darkness and evil rise to do battle with those of the light and the good. Further, it is that curious pivotal moment of the twenty-four-hour day, neither day nor night, when darkness and light confront one another, and the one must yield to the other. Thus, within its frame of reference, the twenty-four hours that constitute a day, it is again that decisive single point in time which marks both end and beginning, past and future, death and birth, the all-important single moment in the midst of rushing time which so fascinates Gryphius. When all of these associations are realized as part of the meaning of "Mitternacht" in lines five and six, however, the simple word assumes a much more intricate web of connotation. It represents, to be sure, a single given moment of time, that of Christian's birth, which has passed and will never return. At the same time, however, it is the ever-recurring moment in time measured by man in terms of day and night. Finally, there attaches to the word a kind of timelessness, its meaning grounded in traditional legend and superstition. This meaning is not based merely on the word's accepted function as the name for a point of time in the man-measured day at which a memorable event, Christian's birth, took place, or as the recurrent point in time meaningful for its central position in the day; rather, it goes beyond all worldly significance for man in its reference to that time when supernatural forces break in upon the natural order of the world. And it might perhaps be mentioned in passing that Gryphius, like many another poet and thinker of his day, gives frequent expression elsewhere in his works to the desperate need for maintaining order—political, social, and religious—in the face of what must have seemed galloping forces of chaos.[3] And so the meaning of the word "Nacht" has been expanded connotatively in the octet in preparation for its use in the sestet on quite a different level.

Line nine is the point of major division in the sonnet, by virtue of its established form, but in Gryphius' sonnets the division between octet and sestet is not often so clearly drawn as it is here by means of a shift in content, in tone, and in the use of the word "Nacht." From line nine, although the darkness of the night remains, the outlook upon and the evaluation of this night have changed with the now explicit realization that there exists also day and light, to which the darkness can lead. Although the "Nacht" of lines nine and eleven is still dependent for its meaning on the assumption of the existence of a supernatural realm, we have, however, moved from negative folk-legend and superstition to biblical legend in the person of the angels of God, "die offt bey Nacht erschienen," to instruct, console, and protect man, guiding him out of abysmal darkness. The antithesis is maintained even here, as "Nacht" is set against "Licht" (line ten)—the first mention of light in the sonnet—but the pendulum has swung over, the tone of the words has changed to one of hopeful anticipation. If line nine is

3. Although we cannot investigate the matter here in detail, we note in passing that the seventeenth century's apparent longing for the restoration or re-creation of order and stability is a force that is felt at every turn. Where German letters are concerned, it is as clear a force in the founding of Fruchtbringende Gesellschaft, whose purpose was, after all, to bring order into the language, as in the composition of Martin Opitz's *Buch von der deutschen Poeterei* and much of the poetry that embodied its precepts. The *Poeterei*, a clear attempt to bring new order and precision into a literature which was threatening to dissolve into utter formlessness, goes about its task primarily by seeking to introduce stability of form, beginning with the most fundamental formal elements of poetry—the verse foot and line. As a whole, it works by prescribing and imposing its rules and regulations from above. Thus employing a thoroughly normative approach, it is necessarily little concerned with the organic growth of language and literature from within. Similarly, there can be little doubt that one of the reasons for the enormous popularity of the sonnet in the German literary Baroque as elsewhere was the appeal of that form's inherent qualities of precision, limitation, and ordered stability. E. M. W. Tillyard's *The Elizabethan World Picture* and Basil Willey's *The Seventeenth Century Background* offer interesting discussions of the significance of order at this time, although the emphasis is on English literature and civilization.

taken by itself, "Nacht" appears here again apparently as a unit of time in a simple reference to that part of the twenty-four-hour day when, according to the Bible, the angels of God often appeared to man. But with its opposition to "Licht" in the following line it becomes clear once again that the meaning of the word goes beyond the literal. In the resulting antithesis it must also be understood metaphorically as Christian's life as a human being, out from the darkness of which he is to be led into the light of understanding and service to God. In line eleven "Nacht," the chaos of nonexistence, again assumes a new meaning, while remaining in balance with "Tag." But common to the *Mitternacht* of superstitious legend and the "Nacht" of lines nine and eleven is the absence of the Divine, and so they are linked, despite their varied meanings, by the negative overtones that attach to each.

If we divide the sonnet in the usual manner into two quartets and two tercets, the last tercet is the only segment in which neither "Nacht," "Licht," or "Tag" appears. Instead, for the first and only time in the poem, the concept of time is found. But "Zeiten" of line thirteen is merely a synonym for *Nacht*, its meaning here expanded to denote man's temporal existence, a life of spiritual darkness, passage through which is necessary for attainment of the eternity of an existence with God.[4] Thus the sonnet begins with an antithesis which proceeds from the positive to the negative, but it concludes with that of finite existence and eternity in another world, in which this movement is reversed.

Christian's birth is viewed in this poem from many aspects, but always as a mixture of blessing and tragedy, never free from outside determining forces of one kind or another. The very real tragedy that nearly accompanies his birth takes on a fateful aspect as the poem moves forward. It seems to be merely one more manifestation of the ineluctable outside powers, some friendly, some hostile, which adhere to and direct human life from its beginnings. It is not so much the transitoriness of life that is stressed here and is so disillusioning, as its uncertain, ambiguous, paradoxical qualities, man's ultimate powerlessness to control events here on earth or the direction they will take in the hereafter. Although the tone of the sonnet does change at the beginning of the sestet to a more positive, hopeful outlook, the last tercet remains a prayer for indispensable aid from a higher power. As Leonard Forster has indi-

4. Cf. also Jöns, *Das "Sinnen-Bild,"* pp. 180–83.

cated, stoicism never was able to provide anything like a satisfactory consolation for Gryphius' fears and doubts, and he lacked the confidence necessary for certainty.[5]

The inconstancy of all things mortal and the suddenness of unforewarned change are reflected in this poem by the poet's use of the word "Nacht," the meaning of which changes rapidly and at times unexpectedly in the course of the sonnet. If, for a moment, we consider again its first occurrence in line three, we note that in this instance, taken by itself within its own clause, its meaning is impossible to determine. Not until line five do we learn that Christian was actually born at night, so that "Nacht" of line three can be taken literally. By the end, of the sonnet, however, "Nacht" has lost all claim to a specific meaning, having itself become ambiguous and uncertain, signifying everything from the single moment, in its various senses, to Gryphius' "night of time." The sonnet is written in celebration of his son Christian's birth, but within the short space of its fourteen lines the poet moves from this most personal of concrete experiences to the most general of abstractions, the nature and meaning of life itself. The tensions between becoming and dying, between night and day, between birth and death, between transience and eternity, form the unifying elements of the poem. They are polarities which are all reflected in the *Augenblick*.

5. *The Temper of Seventeenth Century German Literature* (London, 1952).

# 4

## Uber die Geburt Jesu

NAcht mehr den lichte nacht! nacht lichter als der tag /
Nacht heller als die Sonn' / in der das licht gebohren /
Das Gott / der licht / in licht wohnhafftig / ihmb erkohren:
   O nacht / die alle nächt vndt tage trotzen mag.
   O frewdenreiche nacht / in welcher ach vnd klag /
Vnd fünsternüß vnd was sich auff die welt verschworen
Vnd furcht vnd hellen angst vnd schrecken ward verlohren.
   Der himmel bricht! doch felt nuh mehr kein donnerschlag.
Der zeitt vnd nächte schuff ist diese nacht ankommen!
Vnd hatt das recht der zeit / vnd fleisch an sich genommen!
   Vnd vnser fleisch vnd zeitt der ewikeitt vermacht.
Der jammer trübe nacht die schwartze nacht der sünden
Des grabes dunckelheit / mus durch die nacht verschwinden.
   Nacht lichter als der tag; nacht mehr den lichte nacht!
                    (*Werke* 1: 30)

(Night, more than brilliant night! Night, brighter than the
                                   [day!
Night, brighter than the sun, a night on which was born that
                                   [light
Which God, Light of Lights, had chosen as His light.
O night, which proudly can defy all nights and days,
O joy-filled night, on which lament and all our woes,

And darkness, and all that had caballed against our world,
And fright, and fear of Hell and terror were dispatched.
The heavens part, but thunderbolts do no more issue forth.
He who created time and night on this night did appear,
And to himself the bonds of time and flesh adhere,
And to eternal life our time and flesh consign.
The night of aching woe, the blackened night of sin,
The darkness of the grave is through the night defeated.
Night, brighter than the day! Night, more than brilliant
                                         [night!)

As I have attempted to show in my analysis of the sonnet "Auf die
Geburt seines ältesten Sohnes Christiani," the concepts *Nacht, Zeit,*
and *Augenblick* are related to one another in Gryphius' poetry by
more than the fact that they are all expressions of time. Their
meanings often shift, sometimes overlap, and altogether they seem
to possess a far more complex significance for the poet than may
appear at first glance. Each of these words may occur in any one
of several meanings, or more than one meaning may attach to it
simultaneously in any one occurrence. Rather than causing confusion, however, the ambiguity which often results serves only to
enrich the work of which it is a purposeful part. What has already
been said of the images and the variations upon them in the sonnet
treated in chapter two above applies not only to their use in that
individual poem. The concept of time runs through Gryphius' writings, his prose and his drama as well as his poetry, as a thematic
leitmotif. It occurs in both religious and secular contexts, and an
alternate splitting or fusing of the individual time images is frequently found.[1] It is true that the poets of the seventeenth century

    1. Of interest in connection with this aspect of Gryphius' use of imagery
is Albrecht Schöne's discussion in *Säkularisation als sprachbildende Kraft,*
Palaestra, no. 226 (Göttingen, 1958), especially pp. 36 ff. What interests
Schöne particularly in his discussion of the union of three different meanings
in the symbol of the crown in the drama *Carolus Stuardus* is "nicht nur die
Dreistufigkeit seines Sinnbildes, sondern vor allem die *ein*bündige Dreiheit.
Wie der Schauplatz gleichbleibt, zuvor im Palast, dann im Kerker, so legt der Fürst
seine Krone nicht ab, um den Dornenkranz des Märtyrers statt ihrer zu er-
greifen, sondern die Krone bleibt ihm, sie 'verändert,' sie 'vergrössert' sich.
("not only the triple level of this image, but above all the quality of *one*-ness in
this triad. Just as the scene remains the same, at first in the palace, then in the
prison, so, too, the prince does not lay down the regal crown in order to assume the martyr's crown of thorns in its stead. Rather, the same crown remains his; it is 'transformed,' its dimensions are augmented.")
    "Diese Umschlägigkeit des Bildes aber . . . ist nicht auf die Kronen-

are concerned, perhaps to the modern reader inordinately so, with the idea of time and transience, so that we should expect precisely these ideas to be mirrored in Gryphius' works also. But while Margarete Hoerner and Leonard Forster among others are correct in maintaining that in general this century displays an excessive concern for the moment, it is often the intense personal meaning which this and other expressions and images of time seem to have assumed for Gryphius and their function within the structure of his individual poems which set this poet apart from the many of his seventeenth-century contemporaries who make use of essentially similar formulations.[2] Not the frequency of their appearance, then, but the way in which Gryphius turns these images and the purpose for which he uses them is of primary importance. It must, therefore, be regarded as an oversimplification when, for example, Gerhard Fricke, in his compilation of Gryphius' images and his discussion of their application, speaks merely of the particular attractiveness of negative metaphors of darkness, not only to Gryphius, but also to many another Baroque poet, because of their easy adaptability to the formation of antitheses when combined with positive images of light; or when, in commenting on the use of the metaphor "Nacht" in the poem "Über die Geburt Christi," he has this to say: *"Die Geburtsnacht Christi oder die Nacht der eigenen Geburt* verlockt auch hier besonders zu geistreichen antithetischen Wortspielen und zu dem künstlichen Durcheinander von eigentlichem und metaphorischem Sinn, wie etwa in . . . dem Sonett auf Christi Geburtsnacht: 'Die jammer trübe nacht, die schwartze nacht der sünden, / Des grabes dunckelheit mus durch die nacht verschwinden.'"* (*"The night of Christ's birth or that of his own birth* is also especially enticing for witty antithetical puns and the artificial combi-

---

Trias eingeschränkt. Was hier zum ergreifenden Symbol des Trauerspiels erhoben ist, zeigt sich an vielerlei Stellen von eingeschränkterem Funktionsbereich als eine für Gryphius durchaus bezeichnende Stilform. Ihre Voraussetzung und Grundlage liegt in der Entdeckung und Ausnutzung mehr oder vielschichtiger Bedeutungen und Bezüge des gleichen Wortes" (p. 48). "This reversibility of the image, however . . . is not limited to the crown triad. What is raised here to a moving symbol for this drama appears in several places in a more limited function as a stylistic device quite characteristic of Gryphius. Its prerequisite and its basis lie in the discovery of the multilevel meanings and references of the same word.")

2. Margarete Hoerner, "Gegenwart und Augenblick. Ein Beitrag zur Geistesgeschichte des 17. und 18. Jahrhunderts," *Deutsche Vierteljahrsschrift* 10 (1932): especially 461, 466 ff.; and Leonard Forster, especially pp. 11–17.

nation of real and metaphysical meaning, as, for example, in . . . the sonnet on the night of Christ's birth: 'The night of aching woe, the blackened night of sin, / The darkness of the grave is through the night defeated.'")[3] Gryphius may be chiefly a poet of the intellect, but even a studied use of rhetoric does not, of itself, cause his poetry to be either wooden or "unpoetic." From the fact that the often subtle turnings of his imagery are obviously well considered does not follow the conclusion that his poetry is superficial or lacking in depth. And, to view Gryphius' use of the image "Nacht" in the sonnet presently before us as nothing more than an example of "geistreichen antithetischen Wortspielen," to speak of embellishment only for its own sake, or to suggest that the poet's goal is only the presentation of the striking intellectual *pointe,* is to do an injustice to a sensitive poet.

It may well be, as Hoerner and Forster have pointed out, that the Baroque view of time is like that of light seen through a prism, the fragmentation of a continuum, and that the main impression made by the idea of time on the seventeenth-century thinker and poet, the aspect of time with which he is most concerned, is the fragmentary *Augenblick,* in contrast to that view of time as a continuous, durative dimension as it appears in the literature of Classicism. But we can accept such generalizations only with caution, not so much because they may not be valid, but because, taken without reference to specific works, they tend in their self-sufficiency to obscure other, more important factors. Both Gryphius and Opitz, for example, show a marked interest within their poetry in the single moment. This similarity between the two is, however, no more than superficial and could never succeed in concealing their differing attitudes toward and reactions to the moment. It would seem that Forster's "rule of thumb," according to which in seventeenth-century poetry the word "Augenblick" can usually be substituted for "Zeit" without greatly altering the sense, has already been proven to be without real foundation with the realization of the complexity of the concepts of time and moment as Gryphius uses them in the sonnet on the birth of Christian. The meanings of these two words are evidently not quite so simple to the poet, and no such one-to-one relationship emerges in his poetry. Miss Hoerner is undoubtedly correct in her conclusion that, as a result of this experience of reality only in and as the moment, the

3. Fricke, pp. 40–42.

Baroque poet can neither know rest in this world nor predict it with confidence for the next; that continuity in time and human experience, which seems to have been lost already when Du Bellay viewed the ruins of Rome, had not yet been replaced. As she states, "Dem kurzen, vergänglichen Augenblick gegenüber stehen Nacht, Tod und Unendlichkeit, deren Erwartung nichts Beruhigendes mit sich bringt. Sie bleiben das unbekannte Land, von dessen Bezirk kein Wandrer wiederkehrt." ("Opposed to the brief, transient moment stand night, death, and infinity, the expectation of which affords no consolation. They remain unknown territory, from within whose confines no traveller ever returns.")[4] It is such a continuity, of a semi-mystical nature, which Gryphius seeks to restore in the sonnet "Über die Geburt Jesu"—an effort supported poetically by the use of familiar images in new patterns and combinations, by well-considered ambiguity and multiplicity of meaning, by the use of rhetoric, and, in particular, by a parallelism which goes beyond the external form of the poem and exists between the syntactical structure of the verse and its content. In short, he makes use of the only means at his disposal, the poetic word in all its many facets.

Time and again Gryphius writes of the *Augenblick*, the single point in time which yet ever returns and, paradoxically, seems to represent constancy in the midst of the unchecked flow of time. I have tried to show in a previous chapter that Gryphius sees in the single moment a fusion of time present and time past, a combination of antithetical and apparently contradictory characteristics which are attributable also to the Divine: "Gott, dem nichts fällt noch kommt / dem alles steht und blüht / Der was noch künfftig ist als gegenwärtig sieht / Wil auch vor Augenblick uns Ewigkeiten geben" (*Werke* 1: 105). And, following the traditional practice so popular with the mystics, by which the inexpressible is in fact expressed by means of paradox, Gryphius, in "Über die Geburt Christi," depicts God in like fashion as that being whose very nature is the fusion of two seemingly antithetically opposed qualities. This fusion also takes place at a single point in time, the moment of Jesus' birth, a moment which is itself a study in the union of paradoxes and contradictions, all of which revolve around Gryphius' two Gods and their ultimate synthesis.

The sonnet begins with a hymn to *Nacht*, a specific night, that

4. Hoerner, p. 467.

of Jesus' birth. The imagery and structure of the first four lines warrant special comment. Already in this first occurrence in the sonnet,
"Nacht" exhibits something of the richness of connotation which it
will develop more fully as the poem progresses. The imagery of the
verse "Nacht mehr denn lichte nacht" is based fundamentally on
the conceptual acceptance and recognition of *Nacht* as a segment
of time measured by the clock, as that part of the twenty-four-hour
day marked by literal darkness perceived through the senses.
"Lichte" also certainly refers to the visual experience of light,
with the reader recalling perhaps, in this context, the customary
dazzling aura of light by which the Divine is surrounded in biblical
descriptions of His appearances to man on earth or even the star
of Bethlehem. Thus at the outset Gryphius presents the reader
with the dominant image and central antithesis of the sonnet,
which is to be expanded and paralleled throughout the lines that
follow, only to return again in the final verse in almost its original
form. It is stated here in terms of the sensible phenomena of light
and darkness. It should be noted that Gryphius does not simply
state the antithesis as it is found in the biblical passage John 1: 1:
"Und das Licht scheinet in der Finsternis, und die Finsternis
habens nicht begriffen." By means of the oxymoron, Gryphius not
only heightens the confrontation of opposites, but also forces a
union of the two. In a sense, the remainder of the sonnet consists
of a justification for and closer explication of this radical combination on its various levels and in its various meanings for man. So
precise, so intense is the purpose of this sonnet that the poem in its
outer form becomes a reflection of its content.

If, then, "lichte nacht" is an attempted fusion, of what is it to
be a union? The image itself transcends the visible phenomena of
light and darkness, for its strength rests upon the simultaneous recognition of the polarity in these terms, as well as upon the intellectual apprehension of the fact that, while darkness and light are
visually perceived determining characteristics of the day, lightness
is at the same time an attribute of the Divine. For, within the context of the poem, the light of the first quartet must be taken in its
traditional Christian-mystical sense, not only as the physical sign of
Divine presence, but as the ultimate characteristic and symbol of
God, who is presented in line three as "licht / in licht wohnhafftig."
Thus Gryphius combines in this first image of the sonnet not merely
the sensible opposites of darkness and light, but also two realms

whose separation had become evident, with increasing distress, during the course of the seventeenth century—the human-earthly, in the natural phenomenon *Nacht,* and the spiritual-Divine, in *Lichte.* But we have still not exhausted the implications of the initial image, for prefigured here is yet another significance which becomes explicit only later in the sonnet and which is based upon yet another meaning of *Nacht.* For above all this is a specific night, an individual point in time at which a historical event, the birth of Jesus, took place. But the light of the Divine is also that which is eternal, and, as a result, here the transitory and the ever-lasting confront one another. Furthermore, if light is the creator and night the created, then man and his God shall also be joined. The union of all of these contrasting pairs is implicit in "lichte nacht," but each will become explicit in the poem as the poet views in all its aspects the meaning for man of such a synthesis. Throughout the sonnet there is a steady movement from the concrete and the natural to the abstract and the transcendental, from the human to the Divine, the temporal to the eternal, and from darkness to light, until all the polarities finally merge as night becomes day.

The movement toward pure light progresses steadily and consistently throughout the first three lines, intensified anew in each of the three comparisons, as the intensity of the light itself is increased, until a culmination is reached in line two, "Nacht heller als die Sonn'." Here the paradox is doubled, as the light surpasses in strength that of the source itself of all light, the sun. With this step Gryphius moves beyond the physical world and into the realm of the Divine. Correspondingly, "nacht" gradually disappears from these lines, referred to by pronoun only in the second half of line two, and no longer present at all in line three. Although the relative clause of lines two and three refers still to that "Nacht" at the beginning of line two, the light has grown so bright as to envelop the darkness completely. The introduction of the Divine is accomplished by one final intensification of the light, "licht / in licht wohnhafftig," the exaltation of God as the ultimate, absolute light, admitting of no darkness.

The opening words of line four, "O nacht," return the reader to an awareness of the original antithesis, but the confrontation has changed. Gone from "nacht" is all conceptual reference to sense perception in space. "Nacht" is not darkness, but time. It is one individual night, one among many, which has passed like countless others before it, but it is also the night of Jesus' birth. As a result, touched by the Divine and the eternal, the single transitory night is lent, paradoxically, a kind of permanence that raises it above the mere historical. Only thus, as in line four, "O nacht / die alle nächt' vndt tage trotzen mag," where "nächt' vndt tage" represent the entire sum of created time, can this night stand in defiant opposition to the rush of time itself. And so, finally, we are presented with the union of one specific night, a passing unit of time, and the eternal. Gryphius does not use the word "Zeit," however. By substituting instead the phrase "nächt' vndt tage," he is able, through a kind of linguistic counterpoint, to create in the one line three antitheses, each one of which has its separate identity, all of which, however, are linked at one point, so that the first forms a part of the second, the second a part of the third. The word "Nacht" in its first occurrence in the line contains within itself the above-mentioned elements of the transitory unit of time and the eternal. At the same time, as a single night it stands against "nächt' vndt tage," time itself; and in the phrase "nächt' vndt tage" taken by itself, Gryphius is able to keep before the reader, on the surface at least, the original paradox, that combination of light and darkness first encountered in the introductory image of line one, "lichte nacht."

Along with the expansion of the image "lichte nacht" and the rising enthusiasm of the lines caused by the increasing intensity of the comparisons that accompanies the movement away from the earthly and toward the Divine, there is a concurrent and complementary expansion from the standpoint of form. This expansion is manifested in a gradual syntactical and grammatical loosening of the lines, so that a movement takes place from a tight and closed structure to an open, freely flowing sentence form. For the expression of ideas whose effectiveness depends on their conciseness and on the appearance they are meant to give of an unstudied abruptness born of emotion and enthusiasm, Gryphius employs exclamations in the first seven lines. If the first half of line one is compared with the following two half-lines and then these latter, in turn, are compared with the one and one-half lines following them, a terseness of expression is noted, at its most extreme in the first half-line, an abruptness and tautness of form caused primarily by the use of three staccato half-lines in unrelieved sequence. In addition, the comparisons within all three half-lines are closed, i.e., they consist of self-contained, static images, lacking even a verb, which lead to no further modification or description beyond themselves. Even between the first half-line and the two that directly follow there is some loosening in form and rhythm. Here the compressed manner of expression which was employed in the terse juxtaposition of the oxymoron "lichte nacht" is already yielding somewhat in the more extended similes "lichter als der tag" and "heller als die Sonn'." The caesura, until now well-defined and exactly placed in its mandatory position, does not conflict with the rhythm of the lines, which are read with a natural pause after the third foot. The strict adherence to this element of the meter is thus emphasized. It is only after the third half-line in the middle of line two, however, where the transition from the earthly to the Divine begins, that a more striking example of the trend toward a looser, more open form and a more smoothly flowing verse can be seen. Line two is not end-stopped, as is line one, nor does it follow the pattern established in the first three half-lines of concise, self-contained images. Instead, paralleling the expansion in the movement toward the transcendental, a structural expansion begins with the use of the first detailed modifier of "nacht," the relative clause "in der das licht gebohren." The three relative clauses of the next two lines combine with it to produce an opening up of the form. The result is an outward flowing and dynamic quality of the description in contrast to the previous static imagery. Furthermore, in line three, in keeping with the expansion of both form and content, the rhythm of the verse pushes on beyond a third-foot ceasura, which is actually displaced to a position after the fifth foot. With only the one early pause after the first foot, line four (the most dynamic of the quartet) moves on swiftly, without stopping, to its completion.

The first three lines of the second quartet concern explicitly what is only hinted at above, the meaning of this "lichte nacht" for man. For the first time in the sonnet, a direct link is established between man and this night. The connection is indicated by the use of the adjective "freudenreiche," the first modifier of "nacht" that relates to man, expressing human emotion and, at the same time, a value judgment. In lines five through seven the structural loosening and the attendant movement toward expansion in open, smoothly flowing verse continues and reaches its peak. The sequence of substantive "nacht" modified by a relative clause is maintained, but the single relative clause beginning in line five extends over two and one-half lines. Lines five through seven offer the most complete and pronounced contrast to lines one and two, as the four-fold repetition of the proclitic "vnd," loosely linking the members of a series arranged in order of increasing intensity, produces a verse with an inherent forward movement. It fairly surges ahead, carried on by its own momentum. The first enjambements of the poem occur in lines five and six; one line rushes on to the next, until a complete stop is achieved at the end of line seven. Indeed, the caesura in this last line seems to have been completely overcome by the unconstrained forward movement of the lines.

The final line of the octet at once looks forward to what is to come in the sestet and back at the preceding seven lines. It thus separates—and joins—the two major sections of the poem in exactly the manner prescribed by the sonnet form. It is the pivotal center of the poem, set off by its form as well as its meaning. If line eight cannot be called the climax of the sonnet, it clearly embodies the central thought of the poem. Gryphius states here the one great paradox, and the one great union, upon which the meaning of the sonnet depends: the union of the two Gods, the old and the new.[5] The heavens open in line eight, as they do many times in the Old Testament reports, but instead of the Old Testament God of jealousy and wrath appearing with lightning and thunderbolts ready to hurl down upon the sinful, on this night it is the God of love and mercy who is revealed in all the brightness of His glory.[6]

5. Gryphius makes a clear distinction in his poetry between two Gods, apparently the Hebrew God Jahweh of the Old Testament, and Jesus the Son of the New Testament, both of whom seem still to direct events on earth in what appears at times to be a kind of rivalry. Cf. "der ernste Gott," in "Gedencket an Loths Weib," *Werke* 1: 33; "Der strenge richter" in "Grabschrifft eines vortrefflichen Juristen," *Werke* 1: 43. Cf. the statement of the same paradox in lines nine and ten of "Auf die Geburts-Nacht des Herrn Jesu": "Der mit dem Donner um sich schlägt / Wird in die Windeln eingelegt" (*Werke* 3: 114).

6. The combination of the statement "Der himmel bricht!" and the following "Donnerschlag" is an interesting one in connection with Gryphius' two Gods, and the meaning of the verse must be derived from other uses of these elements by the poet, as well as from their biblical uses. *Deutsches Wörterbuch* (*DWB*) lists both "der Himmel bricht" and "die Wolken brechen sich," without reference, but in each of the two cases the verb is taken in the sense of "aufklären," i.e., there is a clearing up of bad weather, after which the sun shines once more. Obviously this is not the meaning of our line eight, else the joining of the two clauses by the adverb "doch" makes no sense at all. Thunder and lightning appear frequently in Gryphius' poetry, usually as a

This is not to say that the one God has been replaced by the other, but rather that the two have on this night come together, the one flowing into the other, so that a new dimension is added to the Old Testament Jahweh. Gryphius' poetry is replete with the fearful and often inexplicable acts of his "zornige Gott." There is no need, however, to go as far as Curt von Faber du Faur, who sees an unhealable breach between the poet and his God.[7] Despite everything, there also is always hope, since as a result of the union of the two Gods a twofold continuity has been established, in the fusion of the Divine and what is of the earth, as described in the octet, and in that of the Divine and man, depicted in the sestet.

By its form, too, line eight is set off and emphasized. In contrast to the enthusiastic exclamations of the first seven lines, it is the first simple statement of the sonnet. After the climax reached in the unrestricted flow of line seven, it is all the more prominent for its calm statement of fact. With their epigrammatic explanation of the preceding seven lines, line eight's two short clauses indicate a formal restraint which is missing from the remainder of the octet. The three lines which follow the eighth do not move as swiftly as five, six, and seven, but they do resemble them structurally and in tempo and they represent a shift away from the directness and economy of expression of line eight. In contrast to the long, rhetorical hymn of praise that comprises lines five through seven and nine through eleven, there is an intellectual firmness about line eight. These things, together with an unexpectedly early and heavy caesura after the second foot, combine to slow the reading of the two sparse, self-contained statements of line eight and cause the line to stand out in relief. The reader must pause here to pursue the thought just completed, rather than proceed immediately.

---

sign of Divine punishment, though occasionally without specific reference to God, both here on earth and in anticipation of the Day of Judgment. Both ideas, the opening up of the heavens and the thunderbolt, are so closely related to the concept of God in the Old Testament as to be unmistakable. There, God usually appears in a cloud or as the clouds part, and lightning and thunderbolt are normal means of punishment or at the least a sign of the wrath of this Old Testament God, whose very voice is likened to a peal of thunder and whose appearance is likely to be accompanied by it. Cf. God's appearance in a cloud with thunder and lightning in Exodus 19: 16, and more especially Psalms 18: 11: "Vom Glanz vor ihm trennten sich die Wolken, mit Hagel und Blitzen. Und der Herr donnerte im Himmel, und der Höchste ließ seinen Donner aus mit Hagel und Blitzen. Er schoß seine Strahlen, und zerstreute sie, er ließ sehr blitzen, und schreckte sie."

7. "Andreas Gryphius: Der Rebell," *PMLA* 74 (1959): 18.

If the octet is primarily devoted to one of the aspects of the image "lichte nacht," the coming of the Divine to earth and the fusion of these two realms in the person of Jesus, the sestet goes on to fulfill the meaning of this introductory image, treating other implications of the image, which are completely realized only in these last six lines. The sestet deals with the fusion of the Divine with man, and above all with the joining, in man, of the temporal and the eternal, which follow ultimately from the union of the two Gods presented in line eight.

The emphasis in the sestet is on time. The coming of the Divine to earth and the wedding of the two in line nine, the union of God and man in lines ten and eleven, as well as the end result of their coalescence in lines twelve and thirteen, are all stated in terms of time, "nacht," "zeitt," and "ewikeitt." The antitheses of the octet, "lichte nacht," "nächt' vndt tage," based upon the opposition of light and darkness, have yielded here to "zeitt vnd nächte," "nächte . . . nacht," and "zeitt . . . ewikeitt," all based upon a dimension of time. "Zeitt" and "ewikeitt" appear for the first time and frequently thereafter in the sestet; "nacht," which also occurs repeatedly in lines nine through thirteen, has lost all connotation of a visually perceived darkness. Both God and Jesus are characterized in the first quartet as "licht," while the Divine in line nine is "Der zeitt vnd nächte schuff. . . ." But what is the role of "nacht" in these lines, and in what meanings is it used here? "Nächte" of line nine is actually a synonym for *Zeit*, the span of duration of the created world. By its use, a three-fold antithesis, much like that of line four, is produced. Just as "zeitt," the entire body of time, and "nächte," the individual nights taken together, stand opposed, so do "nächte" and "nacht," and finally, "zeitt vnd nächte" and "nacht." *Nacht* is, of course, a unit of time measured by the clock, but also, as that specific time at which a historical event took place, it is actually the individual moment in time, the *Augenblick*; and it is *Nacht* as the moment of Jesus' birth that is here all important. Here then, that which is beyond time, the eternal, breaks through into the finite time of the material world, so that both are joined in "nacht," the moment of the birth of Jesus. And so it is that from the union of the Divine and the human in the person of Jesus, man becomes the connecting link between time and eternity, as, in lines ten and eleven, "zeitt" flows into "ewikeitt," connected to it by "fleisch."

In lines twelve and thirteen the miracle has come to pass, the night has become day as the darkness vanishes. In the meantime, the meaning of the word "nacht" has again shifted. Having fulfilled the movement away from night as visually apprehended darkness, "nacht" of line twelve can be taken only as an abstract, its darkness purely as metaphor, as is indicated by its descriptive modifiers in both lines twelve and thirteen. The meaning of time still attaches to the word "nacht," but in a different sense from the use of "nächte" as a synonym for *Zeit* in line nine and the use of "zeitt" itself in lines ten and eleven. While "zeitt vnd nächte" of line nine is absolute time objectified, time as duration without reference to points or periods, "zeitt" of lines ten and eleven, opposed in the lines to "ewikeitt," is finite time, the duration of life on earth as contrasted to a future life. Only in lines twelve and thirteen, however, do the concepts of sin and salvation appear. Paradoxically, the one night is to vanish here by means of another, but it is important to understand how the word "verschwinden" is to be taken, just how the night will disappear. For it will vanish only in the sense that each night on earth vanishes with the coming of daybreak; that is, there is a fusion of the two, night and day, darkness and light, such that the night is inseparably joined to and regularly flows into its complement, day. In like manner, "nacht," the misery of transitory earthly existence as it is linked inextricably to sin, will "vanish," as the finite flows into the infinite in a union brought about in and through the single point in time, the moment of Jesus' birth, when man and the Divine, the temporal and the eternal, joined, in a moment which has passed into the flux of time and which is yet everlasting.[8]

In this sonnet Gryphius celebrates the birth of Christ. In his poetry, where again and again there is an attempt to combine these apparently separated entities, the poet testifies to his awareness of the growing breach between the spiritual and the material, the temporal and the eternal, between man and his God. There is no titanism in Gryphius, who will not have man become Divine. He seeks no union with God in this sense. There is no hint of conflict,

---

8. Albrecht Weber, in a brief but interesting article, "*Lux in tenebris lucet*. Zu Andreas Gryphius' 'Über die Geburt Jesus,' " *Wirkendes Wort* 7, no. 1 (1956/57): 13–16, notes the paradox inherent in the historical event and that which is ahistorical in Jesus' birth. Although he recognizes also the type of fusion manifested in the second tercet, likening it to the movement in the calendar day, he does not concern himself with the idea of the moment in this sonnet as it has been discussed above.

only a calm in his goal, a union where the one can blend into and thus merge with the other, as in a circle, where each segment of the line flows into the next, resulting in a continuous whole, an unbroken cycle. Of central importance in the poem is the union of the two Gods in line eight, whence come all other syntheses and without which none would be possible. The sonnet is so balanced as to revolve around this eighth line and thereby emphasize it the more, with the result that the poem itself takes on a circular form which parallels its goal of unbroken circular continuity. The three opening praises of *Nacht* in terms of light in the first two lines show ever-increasing intensity and are paralleled by the three descriptions of night in terms of darkness in lines twelve and thirteen, which show a similar rising movement to a climax in the last member of the series. Moving closer to the center of the sonnet, we find that lines five through seven are parallel in form to lines nine through eleven, notably in the use of the conjunction "vnd" to connect loosely the members of the series and in the resulting effect of an intense forward movement common to both sets of lines, by which the reader is driven constantly onward. In contrast to this, as has been mentioned above, line eight is conspicuous by its brevity and conciseness, its self-contained summation and explanation. Finally, line fourteen is almost an exact repetition of line one, but the only difference is an important one for the form of the poem. In the last line the order of the phrases as they stand in line one has been reversed, so that with the completion of this final line the reader is returned exactly to the beginning of the sonnet, completing the circle. As a result of all this, line eight stands by itself, in form and meaning, in a position which is not without its own significance, for it is as close as is physically possible to the exact center of the poem.

The paradox which is the foundation of the sonnet has been worked into the language so completely that form and content are equal. The unity of the poem rests on the shifting values and functions of the image "Nacht." Its meanings are employed in a way far more subtle and complex than is the simple antithetical *Wortspiel* as it is found elsewhere in Gryphius and in other authors throughout the seventeenth century. If we could say no more of Gryphius' imagery in this sonnet than that he utilizes his recognition of the several meanings and levels of meaning of the word "Nacht" to form striking antitheses which, to be sure, do lend the sonnet an ex-

ternal gloss, this aspect of his style would appear likely to remain
on the level of the witty diversion, an exercise in seventeenth-
century rhetoric. But the purpose of the meaning shifts and antitheses here is neither external embellishment nor the artificial
virtuosity of the intellectually appreciated *Wortspiel*. Rather, the
antitheses and meaning changes are a functional part of the
poem, serving to reflect, from the standpoint of form and rhetoric,
the goal of the poem. The poet begins with an apparently simple
and specific image, which is clear to the reader from the very title
of the sonnet and which is stressed from beginning to end, reinforced particularly by the effective use of assonance and ana-
phora. The complexities of this image, however, become clear only
after the several meanings of "nacht" are revealed in the poem.
The meaning of "nacht" does not change in quite the same way as
does that of "strick" in the passage cited by Schöne in his discussion
of this subject, for there the one word carries out two different
functions by means of its two different meanings at two different
times.[9] Here the various meanings are present from the beginning,
needing only to be unravelled for us like a ball of twine. The resulting change in meaning is cumulative: while each new facet of
the word's meaning is recognized and accepted, the former significance is yet retained. In line twelve, for example, "Der jammer
trübe nacht," the precise meaning of "nacht" may be momentarily
unclear, until a reading of the remainder of the line indicates that

---

9. Commenting on the reversibility of many of Gryphius' images,
Schöne uses as an example an epigram, "Grabschrift eines gehenckten Seilers"
("Epitaph of a Hanged Rope-Maker"): "Was diesen leib erhält; kan oft den
leib verterben / Ich lebte von dem strick / und must am strick ersterben."
("That which maintains this life can often life destroy: / By the rope I lived,
and by it had to die.") He then goes on to point out: "Der Strick als Produkt
und Lebensunterhalt des Seilers einerseits, als Hinrichtungswerkzeug anderer-
seits wird in seiner umschlägigen Funktion noch dadurch gesteigert, daß seine
vor der Aufspaltung in entgegengesetzte Wirkungen vorhandene, im gleichlau-
tigen Wort bewahrte Einsinnigkeit sich noch auf das gleichartige Objekt hin
fortsetzt und erst dann ins Positive und Negative auseinanderfaltet: derselbe
Strick wirkt auf denselben Leib—gibt ihm erst Leben und dann den Tod."
("The function of the rope as the product and source of support for the rope-
maker on the one hand, as the tool of his execution on the other hand, is
heightened in its reversible quality by the fact that the unequivocal nature of
its meaning, which is preserved before the division into opposite effects by the
use of the same word, is further extended to the same object. Only then do its
positive and negative meanings unfold: the same rope affects the same body—
gives it first life, and then death.") (Schöne, p. 49).

10. Even though "nacht" functions as a metaphor for human existence

the word is to be taken metaphorically.[10] The result is something of a paradox. As "nacht" takes on its various connotations, it necessarily becomes more vague in its denotation, and the question of its exact meaning becomes less clear with every step. Yet its meaning for the reader, and the meaning of the sonnet, thereby become richer. Line fourteen is the same as line one—and yet it is not the same, just as "nacht" of line fourteen is the same as "nacht" of line one, and yet after its occurrence in many different meanings in the preceding thirteen lines, it is very different.

It has already been mentioned that among the various time-images he uses, Gryphius is particularly fascinated by the word "Nacht." "Über die Geburt Jesu" offers a provocative study of the word, both in its relationship to other images of time and in its own many meanings for the poet. These meanings are so presented that, when the last line is read, all of them must finally be considered together.

---

in this first of three parallel phrases, it remains ambiguous until the last two members of the series are read.

# 5

# Abend

DEr schnelle Tag ist hin / die Nacht schwingt ihre fahn /
Vnd führt die Sternen auff. Der Menschen müde scharen
Verlassen feld vnd werck / Wo Thier vnd Vögel waren
   Trawrt jtzt die Einsamkeit. Wie ist die zeit verthan!
   Der port naht mehr vnd mehr sich / zu der glieder Kahn.
Gleich wie diß licht verfiel / so wird in wenig Jahren
Ich / du / vnd was man hat / vnd was man siht / hinfahren.
   Diß Leben kömmt mir vor alß eine renne bahn.
Laß höchster Gott mich doch nicht auff dem Laufplatz
                              [gleiten /
Laß mich nicht ach / nicht pracht / nicht lust / nicht angst
                              [verleiten.
   Dein ewig heller glantz sey vor vnd neben mir /
Laß / wenn der müde Leib entschläfft / die Seele wachen
Vnd wenn der letzte Tag wird mit mir abend machen /
   So reiß mich auß dem thal der Finsternuß zu Dir.
                      (*Werke* 1: 66)

(The rapid day is done. Night unfurls her banner
And leads the stars on high. The weary troops of men
Abandon field and work. Where birds and beasts once roamed,
Now solitude stands grieving. How fleeting time is wasted!

68

The skiff of limbs draws slowly near the final port.
Just as this light expired, so in a few scant years
I, you, and what we own, and what we see, shall vanish.
Life seems to me to be much like a running track.
Almighty God, let me not slip upon the course!
Let me not woe nor pomp, nor joy nor fear mislead!
Let, when the weary body falls asleep, the soul awaken,
And when on that last day my evening too is nigh,
Then snatch me from this vale of darkness to Thyself.)

It is quite possible that no other single poem by Gryphius displays
so clearly both his greatness and his limitations as "Abend," the
third of the cycle of four "time of day" sonnets which introduce the
second book in the Szyrocki edition. In this one poem we are simultaneously aware of Gryphius' unbreakable ties to the age of which
he is so prominent a representative and of the signs within his
poetry which presage the coming of the young Goethe and an entirely different type of lyric. We are aware of his mastery of the
sonnet form, and of his variations on and contributions to that
form, of his respect for and acceptance of the literary traditions of
the seventeenth century, and, at the same time, of a striving for
originality and the expression of the unchecked surge of his own
feelings. Nor would it be easy to find more clearly or succinctly
stated among his poems his views on the fate of man and on his
relationship to the world about him and to God. That Gryphius
chose to write a sonnet entitled "Abend" is not in itself surprising,
in view of his obvious predilection for and success with the sonnet
form and of the long tradition of the *Abendlied* in Western literature, a current which winds its way through all of German literature, extending to contemporary poetry. What is of interest here,
however, is how Gryphius applies to this tradition his own particular poetic skill and genius and how he makes use of the sonnet
form. It is a question, then, of how the individual poet deals with
two such already existing factors as theme and fixed form, which
stand ready at his disposal and, consequently, must become to
some extent external determinants of his poem, in order for him to
arrive nevertheless at a unique poetic creation. The discussion
which follows is concerned primarily with noting the distinguishing
characteristics of this poem, determining how the poem works, and
deciding whether it is in fact artistically successful.

It soon becomes clear from a reading of "Abend" that it is

neither a typical *Abendlied* nor a typical sonnet, even though, particularly in terms of the method used by the poet and the poem's ultimate purpose, its position in the literary Baroque could not be mistaken. Erich Hofacker has pointed out correctly that the great majority of German *Abendlieder* are set against the backdrop of the traditional calm of evening.[1] Evening is, after all, normally viewed as the time for rest from the hectic activities of the day, a time of peaceful repose and security of a kind that can really be achieved only with the return home after the day's work has been completed. At first glance, the weary men who leave their work in the fields at day's end in the opening quatrain of the sonnet might well be headed for such peace and comfort in their homes. The picture presented in the first three and one-half lines seems to be— and should be—one of calm, a still landscape. It is an empty scene, devoid of life except for the slowly moving men, who are themselves in the process of leaving. This evening, however, will yield no solace to the troubled speaker of the poem. On the verbal level, we find the sonnet producing a melody that runs contrapuntal to the anticipated tranquility of evening, the very antithesis of stillness. Conceptually, the landscape itself has come alive. There is a sense of movement that already in the first two lines belies the possibility of rest. Thus immediately a tension is evoked, in form and content, which pervades the entire sonnet. It is far from being a still landscape, for all that should be at rest is filled with motion. While we might expect to find the day described in terms of its length, perhaps "Der kurze tag," the poet views it instead as a swiftly moving thing, "Der schnelle tag ist hin. . . ." Night does not gradually descend upon or envelop the earth, but, the only real actor in the quartet, unfurls its banner and leads the stars aloft in a military march. Even the verb "verthan," which closes these four lines, besides its meaning of "wasted," contains also the idea of something that has vanished, passed away. In a sense, the images of the quartet have been inverted. That which is normally passive or gradual has become active and abrupt, while the living beings in the landscape act only negatively, if at all. The solitude that results from the close of this day's activity, far from having a soothing, consoling effect, contributes only to a kind of melancholy with which everything is bathed: "wo Thier vnd Vögel waren / Trawrt jtzt die Einsamkeit."

1. "Volkscharacter und Lyrik," *Monatshefte* 21 (1929): 188–89.

Despite this underlying sense of motion, the first three and one-half lines of the sonnet remain the depiction of a landscape, a picture of day's end reported by a speaker who acts as observer and narrator, but remains outside his scene. In the second half of line four, however, the description is abruptly interrupted. Leaving the concrete details of the natural world that lies before him, the speaker, in a moment of reflection, reacts directly to it. But in doing so he becomes a part of his picture and shatters any semblance of objective description that still remains. We are at once aware that the landscape is not the poet's primary concern, but what he sees imposed upon the ordinarily calm, ordered natural world from without, the powerful force of time. Now also the reason for the intense motion and the veil of melancholy of the first quartet becomes clear, for the movement is nothing else than that of swiftly passing time seen as an active force, the poetic attempt to make the concept of transitoriness accessible to the senses. The significance to Gryphius of time and transience has been abundantly treated elsewhere, and any detailed recapitulation here of this matter would serve no purpose. Let it suffice to say that time, as an absolute and terrifyingly active negative force in the world is one of the most striking images in Gryphius' writings. The curse of time, in Gerhard Fricke's view, has replaced for Gryphius the curse of sin.[2] In the drama *Carolus Stuardus,* for example, time itself will discover the letter of the king which is to form the basis of the accusations against him and serve to justify his death:

*Cromwell*
Wisst ihr des römschen Briefes Geheimniss nicht zu finden?
*Gesanter*
Wie, dass ihr den gekrönt, der solche Briefe schrieb?
*Cromwell*
Weil das verblümte Stück viel Jahr verdunkelt blieb!
*Gesanter*
Viel Jahr verdunkelt blieb? Wer hat das nun entdecket?
*Cromwell*
Die Zeit, welch aus der Gruft was dunkel auferwecket.

*Cromwell*
(Do you not know the secret of the Roman letter?

2. *Die Bildlichkeit,* p. 116.

*Envoy*
How is it that you gave the crown to one who wrote such
[letters?
*Cromwell*
Because, written in secret, it remained hidden for many years.
*Envoy*
Hidden for many years? Who was it that discovered it now?
*Cromwell*
Time, which wakens secret things even from the grave.)[3]

At the conclusion of the play, vengeance appears on stage in the guise of time, who will punish man in the future for his transgressions. In fact, the passage of time makes up the entire action of the play, if this can be called action.

It is not necessary to review here the seventeenth-century poet's relationship to the natural world or the theorist's view of the role of nature and the imitation of nature in poetry in order to recognize what takes place between the two quartets of this sonnet and how the poet is going about his business of poetry.[4] It would do to recall, however, that perhaps the main reason for the Baroque poet's inability to produce the impression of that kind of Goethean *beseelte Natur* with which we are all familiar lies not in inadequate poetic skill and ability, but rather in his radically different purpose in describing nature. The poet must necessarily begin with a representation of the natural world as he is aware of it through the senses, because it is the only way to his goal. The goal, however, is not the description of the empirical world with any intent to imitate it, but the recognition and the imitation of the ideas and the wisdom which, although incomplete and perhaps only partly visible, do in fact lie behind the material objects of this world. Knowledge proceeds from the senses, which are, however, merely guides to a higher reality. Poetry, then, does not aim at a reproduction of the external appearances of things, but at the disclosure of realities

3. *Andreas Gryphius: Werke in drei Bänden mit Ergänzungsband,* ed. Hermann Palm, vol. 2, p. 429, in Bibliothek des literarischen Vereins in Stuttgart, vols. 169–71 (unaltered photographic reprint of the Tübingen edition, 1884; Hildesheim, 1961).

4. For an informative discussion of Opitz' concept of the "imitation of nature" and its sources, see Herbert Mainusch, "Dichtung als Nachahmung. Ein Beitrag zum Verständnis der Renaissancepoetik," *GRM* 41 (1960): 122–38.

that exist within them. Like the Bible, so too the Book of Nature is regarded as a Divine revelation, clothed in symbols which the poet must decipher for his audience. Nature holds a meaning which the poet is able to transfer into a message for us. Thus the poet cannot be a creator of poetry in the modern sense of the word, and nature is not of interest for its own sake, but only for the truth which it can reveal. This mode of thought, which tends to seek correspondences and symbolical relationships among all things, is manifest, too, in the ideas of mystical philosophers such as Böhme, whose theory of the *Signatur der Dinge* bears its mark. To it can also be attributed at least in part the great popularity in the seventeenth century of emblem literature, which works on basically the same principle of deciphering meanings through the discovery (in the older meaning of *inventio*) of often obscure correspondences.[5] It is of immediate interest because of its relevance to that type of composition of poetry by analogy which serves Gryphius in the sonnet "Abend."

The narrator's sudden exclamation in the second half of line four links the two quartets and at the same time clarifies the relationship between speaker and landscape. After the initial description of the first four lines and the poet's reaction to the natural world, he turns away and proceeds to abstract from it that meaning which it holds for his readers and for all men. With consummately effective control which yields a gradually rising intensity of awareness and of involvement, the poet, in a momentarily ambiguous statement about man and death in line five, coupled with an extended simile which sustains the tension until the climax of line seven, abandons the natural world *qua* natural world and leads into the existential problem of life and death. The "zeit" of line four, which there represents the span of the day just coming to a close, does not reappear in the second quartet, where Gryphius focuses his thoughts on the all-consuming flow of time rather than any one specific day. The concrete landscape of the first four lines is gone, and it becomes clear in retrospect that "Abend" of the title is a metaphor for approaching death and that "zeit" of line four really represents also the period of man's life. Although we speak of becoming aware of new values for these images "in retrospect," as

5. Cf. Mario Praz, *Studies in Seventeenth-Century Imagery* (London, 1947); Rosemary Freeman, *English Emblem Books* (London, 1948); and Albrecht Schöne, *Emblematik und Drama im Zeitalter des Barock* (München, 1964).

we move in time and space from one quartet to the next, they are present together from the beginning, like trains traveling on parallel tracks. Had Gryphius chosen to compose an emblem, the first quartet could be replaced without change in content by a graphic representation of what is stated there. The second quartet, unchanged, could serve as the epigram.

If the "real" natural world of lines one through four has disappeared by line five, the second quartet nevertheless displays the same type of inverted imagery and the same emphasis on movement. The light of line six does not gently fade away, nor does darkness descend gradually—instead, the light disintegrates. Most interesting, however, for its structure and for its expression of the degree to which the normal order of things has been reversed in the poet's eyes, is the well-known line five. Here for the first time in the sonnet the force of time is brought to bear directly upon man, and the futility of his passive position in the face of time's inevitable passage receives its clearest formulation in one striking inverted metaphor. Logically, the line must be read in such a way that the boat is in motion and approaching a stationary port. Grammatically and syntactically, however, the question of whether it is the skiff or the harbor that is in motion in what would otherwise be a fairly common image of approaching death is at least momentarily ambiguous. If the metaphor is to be taken in its traditional sense, then "Der port" must be read as a feminine dative. And indeed, the parallel form *die Porte* did exist along with the more common *der Port*, according to Grimm, although its usage was by no means regular and it apparently was no longer employed after the sixteenth century (*DWB* 7: 2003–4; 2005; 1787–88). It can be assumed that both Gryphius and his readers of the first half of the seventeenth century knew of this second feminine form, even though it may no longer have been in active use by his contemporaries. Further, because of the genitive plural "der glieder," which directly precedes its modified noun, the case of "Kahn" at the end of this line is effectively disguised and can be determined only by context. Finally, according to the alexandrine meter, "zu" would normally be stressed because of its position, and thus the use of an artificial composite "zúnahen" is possible. An ambiguity, then, supported by the reader's familiarity with the usual and therefore partly expected image, by the meter and the lack of complete clarity concerning the case of "der glieder Kahn," as well as by the

existence of the parallel forms *der Port* and *die Porte,* cannot
be denied. But the uncertainty is only temporary, for both the purpose to which the metaphor is put and the context of the lines make
it clear beyond question that "Der port" is a nominative masculine.
Supporting evidence, if needed, is furnished by the fact that in
every other occurrence of *Port* in Gryphius' poetry the noun's
gender, where it can be determined, is masculine.[6] The question
remains: if the ambiguity is assumed and if, in fact, a rather drastic
change in an established metaphor has been intended and carried
through, then to what purpose and with what result for the poem
as a whole?

Gryphius has good reason for the reversal. He is thereby able
to maintain that play and tension between illusion and reality
which has already been introduced in the first strophe of the sonnet
by the apparently paradoxical, simultaneous expression of stillness
and violent motion. By reversing the familiar image of the ship
nearing port, Gryphius divests of its reassuring connotations this
customary symbol of the harbor as a welcome refuge for the lost or
wandering mariner in his storm-tossed ship. The port as a metaphor for death is no longer the often joyfully awaited stopping
place at the end of life's journey, as it is so frequently before, during, and after the seventeenth century for many a traditional
Christian poet with a strong belief in the efficacy of the Divine
power of salvation. Instead, the harbor pursues its victim as if
stalking a helpless prey, deliberately, steadily, inexorably, in a line
which, in contrast to those that precede it, displays neither the
force of abruptness nor the variety of change in inflection or pitch.
The slow but incessant quality of the action described is supported
by the retarding syntactical twist and by the repetition of the long
*a* and extended long *e* sounds. It creeps along to its completion
in a dully frightening near-monotone. And what of the traveler on
this journey? Present he is indeed, not as a passenger, but curiously
fused with the hapless vessel, himself become an object, dehuman-
ized, depersonalized, in fact, fragmented into a bundle of lifeless
limbs, "der glieder Kahn." And as the sonnet progresses, the feeling
increases that something is awry in this world, that not merely the

6. The noun "Port" occurs eleven times in Gryphius' poems, in addition
to occurring in the sonnet "Abend." Twice the gender remains undetermined
for lack of a limiting adjective. In the other nine instances, it is clearly masculine.

images of a poem, but very real things in the world have been reversed, so that it is difficult to distinguish between reality and illusion. The real is only illusion here, while what is actually illusion—the harbor, after all, only *seems* to move—has become terrifyingly real. In this manner the threat of disorder has entered upon the orderly calm of a natural landscape at evening.

It is then a world out of joint—and so closely is form welded to content in the best of Gryphius' lyric that this dominant theme is restated and confirmed by the very form of the octet. Although technically Gryphius employs both the traditional sonnet form and the accepted alexandrine in "Abend," they themselves serve almost to erase the boundary between the reality and illusion of form, for he actually varies and distorts both constantly to such an extent that finally, in the critical line seven, the form temporarily collapses. Enjambements eliminate the pauses at the end of each of the first four lines, and replace them instead at the center of each line, where we would ordinarily expect to find the much more tentative pause of the caesura. The thought in each case then begins in the middle of every line and runs to the middle of the next, an arrangement that produces a kind of laterally sliding movement and contributes to a general imbalance which will not be corrected until the second tercet. The alexandrine is misplaced, off-center. The pause at each half-line marks the end of the colon. One might question whether the first four lines actually comprise a sonnet quartet, or whether they do not in fact form a five-line stanza forced into four-line form, with the first half of line one and the second half of line four really representing the first and fifth lines.

The restlessness of the quartet ends in the second half of line four as abruptly as it began. Line five returns in form to the correctness of the alexandrine, yet the sense of disorder is even stronger here despite the metrical regularity because of the inverted metaphor which has already been discussed above. Line six begins like a normal alexandrine—indeed, at first it appears to be the most regular line of the sonnet yet, its caesura, properly placed after the third foot, paralleling the natural rhythmic pause. The colon, however, does not stop with the line's end, or even at the middle of the following line. Gathering momentum with its forward movement, the thought rushes on unchecked until the end of line seven, which revolts completely against the strictures of the verse form. The disturbed restlessness, hitherto only an undercurrent, finally bursts into the open completely and reaches a climax with the temporary collapse of the meter. After its initial spondee, this strongly proclitic line rushes forward and down in a series of swift one-syllable words. There is no stopping place, nothing that could properly be called a caesura. Although after the first foot the line might technically be scanned as iambic, to do so without qualification would be to do violence to the natural flow of the verse, which supersedes here the mandatory prescription for simple alternation of stressed and unstressed syllables. There is no gradual flow to the rhythm here. It is a halting, almost stumbling rhythm that is twice caught up short and then begins again. A marked disparity in the strength of the various stressed syllables results in a drastic shift away from the precise Opitzian regularity usually associated with this meter. The inflection alternately rises, drops, then rises again, reaching a sustained highpoint with the two heavily stressed words "hat" and "siht." The strong beat of the latter two words diverts attention from and in fact all but eliminates the required stress of "was." This inequality of stress, combined with the extended subject, its parts loosely strung with the proclitic "vnd," and the sequence of one-syllable words, all cause the line to move swiftly toward its conclusion. The pauses in the line, because of the constantly rising inflection, only heighten its forward movement. Gryphius makes clear in the octet that the things of this world, because of their evanescence, are not to be valued; but a calm withdrawal by disengaging himself from them is impossible, for he also recognizes full well that he too is inextricably caught up in the unchecked common flow of all things toward their destruction, and the prospect for a better hereafter is clouded by anxieties.

The last line of the octet is one of childlike simplicity, almost humorous for a moment in its incongruity, even though for Gryphius there could perhaps be no more telling symbol for a life which seemed a constant running. It might be argued that it is a poor line of poetry; there is no doubt that Gryphius could have written a better one. Yet at this point in the sonnet the line fits. It cannot be chance that at precisely the moment when both the accepted form of the sonnet and the speaker himself within the poem have, in a sense, collapsed, the poetic word, too, almost ceases to function. And there is no question that it is a broken man who begins the desperate prayer of the sestet:

Laß höchster Gott mich doch nicht auff dem Laufplatz gleiten /
Laß mich nicht ach / nicht pracht / nicht lust / nicht angst
[verleiten.

Throughout the octet, there is a steady movement from a detached description of the external world to the reactions of one man within that world. Even in line five, where the relevance of the dying day for man is first considered, the idea of death remains still cloaked in metaphor, and the speaker has not yet emerged from behind the third person. Only in lines seven and eight do first-person pronouns appear. No longer able simply to view from a position removed, the speaker of the poem recognizes his own necessary involvement in the world he has depicted. Man is here swept up into the flow of historical events; at the same time the progressive breakdown of the alexandrine and of the sonnet form reaches its most advanced stage. The condition continues into the sestet. In line nine a caesura at the prescribed position after the third foot is impossible if the sense of the line is to be preserved, and the metric pattern has dissolved completely. There is no trace of the regular iambic alternation, unless it be forced unnaturally upon the line, yielding then a meter valid from the standpoint of the written word alone. Similarly, although most of line ten could be formally scanned as alternating iambs, the steady flow of the alexandrine is immeasurably weakened by the staccato beat of the series of heavily stressed one-syllable nouns. New patterns, formed and acting within the line itself—the repetition of "nicht" plus a one-syllable noun, the repeated *ch* sound itself, and the strong *a* assonance—tend to draw attention from and thus generally de-emphasize the basic metric pattern of the verse. What is manifested here is not an esthetic tension between meter and natural accent, but outright conflict, reflecting once again that conflict which has already appeared in earlier lines and which lies at the heart of the poem. In the first tercet, only line three remains intact, that is, a clear, unforced alexandrine. It is no coincidence that this third line, for the first time in the sonnet, expresses the concept of a positive force that transcends the merely earthly. As a unifying element, the "ewig heller glantz" that is the vehicle here for the Divine fulfills the promise of the stars of line two, contrasting temporally with the "schnelle Tag" of line one as well as with the evanescent "licht" of line six.

The general movement within "Abend" is from the restless containment of the first quartet toward a loosening of the bonds, metrical and emotional, in the second four lines. The process culminates with the breakthrough of the personal plea and prayer of the first tercet, accompanied by a corresponding formal breakdown of the verse. These three lines, however, now that at least the possibility of Divine aid has been recognized, close with what is until now the most relaxed single line of the poem. The lines of the second tercet then achieve a kind of balance generally absent from or at the very least severely distorted in the preceding ten lines. The laterally sliding tendency of the lines, which is most apparent in the first quartet, yields finally to a relatively calm stability. For the first time the pairs of opposites "Tag"/"Abend," "mich"/"dir," "Leib"/"Seele," and "entschläfft"/"wachen" appear in a tentative balance. Just as the conflict between an unconstrainable rhythm and formal metric pattern is dissolved, so too the separation between the temporal and the eternal, between the "schnelle Tag" of line one and "ewig heller glantz" of line eleven, seems on the point of being breached by the apparently smooth transition expected from "Leib" to "Seele" in line twelve. If the order and regularity of the alexandrine have already been restored in line eleven, line twelve bears no resemblance at all to the rhythm, tone, and sound of nine and ten. It has nothing about it of the harsh abruptness and strident tone, the insistent rhythmic surge caused in nine and ten by the heavy, sharply delineated accents, the predominance of one-syllable words, and the clipped quality of the consonant combinations. Although line twelve, too, begins with the same heavily stressed "Laß," the pattern of the remainder of the line is radically different. The half-expected parallelism with lines nine and ten fails to materialize. The rhythm is not rigid, does not move in groups of two syllables, as it does in ten. The inflection does not alternately rise and fall sharply with each stressed and unstressed syllable. Instead, after the initial stressed syllable, it rises gradually, with the help of a subordinate clause and a delayed caesura, until the end of the fourth foot, then falls off evenly to the end of the line. This gradual rhythm lends a gentler flow to the line, which is itself of significance as a second turning point in the sonnet. The calm that sets in here is even more pronounced in the following two lines, whose structure, too, reflects the relaxation of the tension that marked most of the first tercet. The syntactical arrangement employed in line twelve, the order of dependent and independent clauses which contributed to that line's easy flow, is here retained, while the stressed first syllable is eliminated. But the clauses are expanded now so that each comprises an entire line, and, as a result, lines thirteen and fourteen are perfectly balanced. With the main stresses falling within the last two feet of line thirteen and in the first foot of line fourteen, the continuously but slowly rising inflection is maintained until it peaks at the end of thirteen and the very beginning of fourteen and then drops unhindered but evenly. The caesura after the third foot of line thirteen is not conspicuous by its strength, and in fourteen it disappears for all practical purposes. The result of this structuring is a distinct smoothness throughout the final tercet which is just as clearly missing from the first eleven lines of the poem. These last three tentatively optimistic lines of the sonnet are a recapitulation, in brief, of the first quartet, raised now to a higher level, which helps to create a symmetry of the whole. But if "Der Menschen müde scharen" are surrounded by the gloom of a melancholy landscape, the "müde Leib" hopefully anticipates the eternal. With the gentler rhythms of the second tercet, a certain stability and balance, and a relative calm, have been achieved. But, though the pairs of opposites have attained a cautious equilibrium, it is by no means a state of absolute rest—this would contradict their very nature. Within that balance there is still the play of dynamic energies. From it there still issues a sense of rupture, of incomplete healing. From it, too, God must still "tear" man unto himself. But measured on the scale of congruence between inner experience and outside reality of a Gryphius, or possibly of the Baroque period itself, perhaps this is all that can be expected.

It may well be the result of the fact that Gryphius' "Abend" is, as A. G. de Capua terms it, a "recognized masterpiece" that it has only rarely been submitted to close critical scrutiny and evaluation.[7] In one such attempt, the poem is deemed an artistic failure. Although he admits that it is probably the best of the four-poem cycle, George Schoolfield is dismayed by what he terms Gryphius' inability to create poetically a still landscape. Because his arguments really go beyond this single poem in their implications and because they represent one view of Baroque poetry still held by

7. "Two Quartets: Sonnet Cycles by Andreas Gryphius," *Monatshefte* 59 (1967): 326.

some, they must be considered here: "Of this series [the four 'time of day' sonnets] 'Abend,' with its noble opening quatrain, is most successful, but the sense of movement is no less evident. At noon it takes the form of flight and search, at evening it becomes slower, a processional, but movement nonetheless. . . . The promise of the quatrain is not fulfilled; the skiff of limbs nears its port, and to the andante of the initial picture is juxtaposed a not too graceful presto —life is like a running track. This simile forms the clumsy joint between octave and sestet. A certain repose is restored with the request that the soul may wake when the body falls asleep and that . . . God will snatch him from the vale of gloom unto himself. We should hope for a gentler movement."[8]

The function of this feverish activity within an ostensibly still landscape has already been discussed above. The judgment that the poem fails because of the intense motion, that is, of a lacking harmony of the whole, is certainly open to question. Nineteenth-century standards are here applied to a seventeenth-century sonnet, and negative criticism based without qualification on such criteria can be a serious breach of method. It must be readily admitted that the poem is no *Stimmungsgedicht,* as the modern reader, steeped in the Romantic-Classical tradition, uses the word. The tone is never lyrical, as this term is used today. But perhaps the difficulty is precisely this, for "Abend" comes so close to being a *Stimmungsgedicht* that we are tempted to treat it as such and to judge it on that basis. Yet in the very fact that a mood is here almost achieved, the great distance between this sonnet and a Romantic "mood poem" becomes all the clearer. For a mood, be it grief, melancholy, or joy, presupposes a *Weltbild* that is somehow uniform, a union or congruity between the expressed feeling and

8. "Motion and Landscape in the Sonnets of Andreas Gryphius," *Monatshefte* 42 (1950): 342. In his wish for a "gentler movement" in the final line of the sonnet, Schoolfield fails to take into consideration the context of this second tercet. In these lines, with the prospect of Divine aid, Gryphius turns to the biblical word. If line twelve is reminiscent of Song of Solomon 5: 2, "Ich schlafe, aber mein Herz wachet," line fourteen contains a clear allusion to Psalms 23: 4, "Und ob ich schon wanderte im finstern Thal. . . ." Similarly, the verb "reißen," though it may sound harsh, is quite common in the Scriptures in such situations where Divine intervention is involved. Clearly there is the feeling that mortal existence, or perhaps the forces of Satan, "holds fast" to man, necessitating a forceful pull. Cf. Job 21: 32, "Er wird dich reißen aus dem weiten Rachen der Angst"; and Psalms 116: 8, "Du hast meine Seele aus dem Tode gerissen." The use of "reißen" in "Abend" is quite in keeping with the biblical overtones and the desperate plea of the line.

the image used to express it. This union is withheld in "Abend,"
which in this respect can stand as an example of Baroque poetry
in general. Neither poet nor reader ever becomes one with the
world depicted. This relationship can perhaps be made clearer if
we compare "Abend" with a poem from a different period, Tieck's
thematically similar "Der Tod" ("Death"):

Wechselnd gehn des Baches Wogen,
Und er fließet immer zu,
Ohne Rast und ohne Ruh
Fühlt er sich hinabgezogen,
Seinem dunklen Abgrund zu.

Also auch des Menschen Leben
Liebe, Tanz und Saft der Reben
Sind die Wellenmelodie,
Sie verstummt spät oder früh.

Ewig gehn die Sterne unter,
Ewig geht die Sonne auf,
Taucht sich rot ins Meer hinunter,
Rot beginnt ihr Tageslauf.

Nicht also des Menschen Leben,
Seine Freuden bleiben aus,
Ist er nur dem Tod gegeben
Er behält ihn dort im dunkeln Haus.

(Ever change the river's wavelets,
And it flows on constantly,
With no rest and with no pause,
It feels itself attracted ever
Downward towards its dark abyss.

So is too the life of man,
Love, dance, and the vineyard's nectar
Are his melody of waves.
It is silenced late or early.

Eternally the stars must set,
Eternally the sun must rise,
Dips its red ball in the ocean,
In red begins its daily course.

Not the same the life of man,
All his pleasures stay behind,
Once delivered to Death's hand,
He resides in Death's dark house.)[9]

Here, too, pairs of opposites lie at the heart of the poem, which centers on the antithesis of man/stars and the supporting contrasts "Leben"/"Tod," "Melodie"/"verstummt," and "rot"/"dunkeln." Yet they combine in the harmony of a regular, symmetrical movement, a rhythmic ebb and flow, which admits a unified mood, a *Stimmung*, a yielding up of the self. It is this yielding which the poet of "Abend" denies.

But to charge the poem and the poet with failure because of this lack of harmony is an error. For once the tacit assumption is rejected that Gryphius in this sonnet consciously attempts but is unable to carry out the description of a motionless landscape, such an interpretation and evaluation loses its cogency. Unity and esthetic integrity do, however, exist in "Abend"—and, paradoxically, that very discrepancy that has been pointed out in criticism of the sonnet, the tension between stillness and agitated motion, plays a significant role in establishing both. For the unity lies not in repose, but in Gryphius' attempt, poetically, to restore some kind of order and balance to a world suddenly bereft of both once the forces of chaos have broken through the surface of things and threaten to dominate. For such a purpose, the closed, self-limiting sonnet form is eminently well suited. The problem is to find meaning where there seems to be no meaning, to balance the destructive forces acting upon man, and above all the awesome, violent, swift-moving forces of time, by some other stabilizing power that possesses the necessary permanence. The result in "Abend" is a final balancing—or at least some hope for a balancing—of the physical by the spiritual, of the life/death cycle in this world by another, enduring life. It is an equilibrium not to be achieved without the active participation of the Divine in this world, the effect of which is manifested not only in the sudden rhythmic calm of the second tercet, but also in the reappearance there, in the form of "Tag"/ "Abend," of the initial antithesis of the first quartet, "Tag"/"Nacht." "Tag" and "Nacht" in line one are separated metrically by the

9. *Ludwig Tiecks ausgewählte Werke in acht Bänden,* ed. Heinrich Welti, vol. 8 (Stuttgart, 1886), p. 228.

strong caesura after the third foot and grammatically by the function of each as subject of its own independent clause. But the mutual independence of the two concepts goes beyond their merely formal isolation. The two statements involving night and day stand without any connection stipulated between them, not even joined by the conjunction "und," which would indicate the least meaningful relationship between the ideas. It is as if the passing of day and the coming of night are two quite unrelated events. Instead of linking the two clauses, the semicolon seems only to increase the separation between them. Thus the most gradual of natural processes, the perceptibly progressive and continuous flow of light into darkness, appears as lacking in continuity, reflecting that want of order and coherence in the world which we have already discussed above as one characteristic element of the sonnet. By analogy, the second natural process of the poem, the movement from life to death, acquires the same spasmodic quality. Life will not fade away, but, like the light of line six, will disintegrate suddenly. But "Tag" and "abend" of line thirteen, despite their positions at opposite ends, are not so separated. The rhythmic flow simply washes over the potentially divisive caesura, and the two concepts, no longer isolated from one another, are joined within the same clause by the verb. The one is the complement of the other and flows into the other, just as life moves gradually into a death which is no longer final. With the restoration of order in this wish projected into the future, the continuity between life, death, and the afterlife has also been restored.

In the first quatrain, Gryphius presents his readers with a picture of a concrete day coming to an end and of the evening that follows. At the same time, however, day and night are allegories for life and death. While the first four lines represent the verbal result of the speaker's observations in the natural world, the second quartet interprets the scene. The tercet comprises his reactions to the perceptions and insights gained in the octave. The seventeenth-century poet finds that he can neither view nature objectively, since it holds too much "meaning" for him, nor feel at one with it in any way. Too uncertain of his own independence, not at all sure of his strength within the world or of his true relationship to it, he finds no rapport with it. So far as Gryphius is concerned, with both his birth and death determined apparently by the whim of inscrutable natural forces, he can feel no sense of union with a nature so unconcerned. Thus the natural landscape becomes merely another emblem from which a lesson is to be read and learned. Predictably, after his encounter with the landscape in the first strophe, the speaker turns not further into, but away from it and into himself for contemplation of the lesson learned. The lack of spiritual contact with the world is reflected, consciously or unconsciously, by the complete separation between the two quatrains. Like man and nature, the two quartets are related—even externally they are connected by the repeated *a* of all eight rhyming syllables. The same idea lies at the center of each stanza; the means of developing this idea are similar, but again, like man and nature, while they run parallel, they never meet.

If the Baroque has been viewed as the first great age of the sonnet in German literature, it could also easily be called the age of the metaphor, that rhetorical device which, occupying a position midway between the indivisibility of symbol and the duality of simile, joins together in a kind of forced union concepts that are never really free of their inclination toward separation. Man, like the metaphor, maintains a precarious, in-between position, held together only with effort. He is both in nature and outside it, in time and outside it. He is not suffused in an all-embracing, completely embraced All, nor does he seem to belong to any order such that a clear line of division could be drawn between him as a human being and the lower creativity. He feels intensely the fact of his commonality with all living creatures, his *Kreatürlichkeit*, but just as intensely he knows that he is more. In "Abend" too the speaker is delivered up to the forces of transience not as an individual, but as *Kreatur*, born along with the rest of creation, a part of it and apparently indistinguishable from it. The problem of "Abend" is not new, nor is the solution offered, but it is given sensitive, powerful, and imaginative treatment by Gryphius. Far from a poetic attempt to capture a landscape, the sonnet is, after all, an evaluation of that precarious position of man in the world, one which Gryphius, it seems, realized and perhaps experienced more fully and painfully than many of his contemporaries. A part of the temporal world and subject to temporal change, man does not attempt to act, to impose his will on the historical world, but is acted upon by forces beyond him, swept up into the current of events that comprise his existence. But Gryphius is never able to view life with the stoicism and seeming self-control of a Fleming, whose detached indifference and self-assuredness make it possible for him to utter to himself the command, "Sei dennoch unverzagt, gib dennoch unver- loren, / Weich' keinem Glücke nicht, steh' höher als der Neid, / Vergnüge dich an dir und acht' es für kein Leid, / Hat sich gleich wider dich Glück, Ort und Zeit verschworen . . ." ("Be nonetheless undaunted, give nothing up for lost, / Yield not to Fortune's whims, stand far above all envy, / Find contentment in your own self, and deem it no cause for sorrow, / Should Fortune, time, and place cabal at once against you").[10] The command in "An Sich" ("To Himself") comes from within, but for Gryphius, to whom in "Abend" man has become more a helpless object than an individual human being, "der glieder Kahn," the self has no power to give commands, but can only pray for help. It would not be too much to say that sometime between the Renaissance and Gryphius' time, individual identity, as we know it, had been lost. Now a "skiff of limbs," now a storm-tossed ship without compass to steer a course by or pilot to guide it—common to these frequently recurring images of man, all variations of the age-old metaphor of the *Schiff- fahrt* as the journey through life, is the fact that the source of moti- vation, of the direction-giving force, lies never within, but outside the individual.

If man is reduced to the position of inactive recipient of forces that act upon him from without, if he is, as Gryphius so often puts it, merely a plaything of incomprehensible powers as harsh and pitiless as they are obscure and paradoxical, whose treatment of man seems capricious, inconsistent, and unjustified, then the pas- sivity of disengagement can only prove insufficient, stoicism well- nigh impossible. More than ever under such circumstances his sole source of assistance for maintaining the necessary fortitude for the endurance of this world—and for keeping that balance which Gry- phius seeks in "Abend"—as well as his only means for salvation in the next, is Divine aid. But Gryphius' main concern seems not to be with whether a merciful God will aid him in his tribulation, but with whether his countless prayers can in fact be answered. In one of the *Sonn-und Feiertagssonette* he combines the biblical report of Christ calming the stormy sea after hearing the pleas of his frightened disciples with the traditional imagery of the ship's

10. *Paul Flemings deutsche Gedichte*, ed. J. M. Lappenberg, vol. 1, p. 472, in Bibliothek des literarischen Vereins in Stuttgart, vol. 82 (Darm- stadt, 1865).

voyage on the ocean of life. The account of the sonnet, however, differs in one significant detail from that of Matthew 8. In the Bible, Jesus awakens, chides his disciples for their lack of faith, but then does calm the waters. In the sonnet, which transforms the real sea voyage and pleas to Jesus for help in an isolated incident of this world into existential and transcendental symbols, there is only one voice; cry out as it may, no answer, no sign of help, is forthcoming. The Jesus of the sonnet remains asleep, or simply deaf to the plea. The poem is not a simple retelling of the Bible passage in the style of Opitz or Heerman, and it is clear that the lyric "Ich" is not meant to represent one of the disciples of Matthew 8. Nor is the omission of precisely this one element a matter of accidental oversight or economy. The undisguised doubt about the likelihood of Divine aid remains unresolved at the poem's conclusion. The vessel appears headed for shipwreck and disaster. A helmsman does not appear.

Bernhard Blume has shown clearly how in eighteenth-century literature man's view of himself and of his relationship to the world and to God is reflected in the variations upon the common motifs of *Schiffahrt* and *Schiffbruch*.[11] His comment elsewhere that, of the seventeenth-century poets, only Gryphius was able to breathe life into this already spent complex of images bequeathed by the Middle Ages is surely valid.[12] Gryphius' use of the image of the foundering ship buffeted by wind and waves certainly exhibits none of the optimism and assurance that the port will be reached intact that such poets as Logau and Spee, for example, generally give voice to. But already at the beginning of the eighteenth century we can detect, however slightly, a change in the use of the ship metaphor, and with it the beginnings of a new view of the self, heralding an independence of the individual which is to be fully realized only later. Günther's "Kummer-Gedanken" ("Troubled Thoughts") affords a good example:

Nun geh' die Sorgen an:
Nun hängt der Himmel nicht mehr voller Geigen:
Der Jugend Wollust-Kahn
Heißt mich ans Land der Kummer-Inseln steigen,

11. "Die Kahnfahrt. Ein Beitrag zur Motivgeschichte des 18. Jahrhunderts," *Euphorion* 81 (1957): 355–84; and "Das Bild des Schiffbruchs in der Romantik," *Jahrbuch der deutschen Schillergesellschaft* 2 (1958): 145–61.
12. "Lebendiger Quell und Flut des Todes," *Arcadia* 1 (1966): 18–30.

Wo tausend Hütten stehn mit Ach und Weh bedeckt,
Wo jeder Abend mich ins Dornen-Bette steckt.

Mein Geist entsetzet sich,
Jedweder Blick allda ist dem Gewissen
Ein scharfer Schlangenstich,
Durch welchen mir die Seele will entfließen;
Jetzt schmeck ich allererst, was die vor Früchte trägt,
Wenn unsre Jugend hat der Wollust Feld geeggt.

Mein Sinn, Gott, die Natur,
Befehlen mir, vor Kranke Heil zu finden:
Wo aber ist die Kur,
Die meine Seelen-Risse soll verbinden:
Kein Mittel schläget an, die Wunden sind zu groß,
Und das Verderben wirft schon über mich sein Los.

Laß mich, o Einsamkeit!
Nun meine Gruft in deinem Schatten haben,
Wo ich das Sünden-Kleid
Der lasterhaften Jugend kann vergraben:
Erkenntnis, wahre Reu, Verdruß und Seelen-Pein,
Die machen allbereit dazu den Leichen-Stein.

(Now my cares begin:
No longer do the heavens sing so sweetly:
Youth's sweet pleasure boat
Bids me disembark on the shores of the isles of troubles,
Where a thousand hovels stand burdened with misery,
Where every evening tucks me in my bed of thorns.

My soul stares in horror,
My conscience feels every sight
As the stinging bite of serpents,
Through which my spirit seeks to slip away.
For the first time I taste what bitter fruits are born,
When wild youth has sown the fields of earthly pleasure.

My mind, God, Nature
Now order me to heal myself:
But where can be the cure
To heal the wounds that my poor soul has suffered:
No medication works, so great the wounds,
Corruption's lot is cast and falls to me.

O solitude! let my grave be placed in your protecting shade,
When I at last can bury
The cloak of sin that clothes my vice-filled youth.
Insight, true remorse, chagrin, and soul's torment,
Of these my epitaph should be composed.)[13]

To be sure, the poem ends with the contemplation of death as the only goal and the gateway to salvation. However, there is a distinction in the ship imagery between Gryphius and Günther: Gryphius *is* the "glieder Kahn," dismantled and driven, more an object than a person. Günther, on the other hand, *rides in* the "Wollust-Kahn." He has chosen incorrectly and sees himself at the wrong goal, but he *has* chosen, just as he himself has sown false seed and reaped a bitter harvest. The passive Gryphius, no harvester, can only liken himself to the "wiesen blum" that is cut down in "Es ist alles eitell." To Günther come valid commands and, if he trembles before the law, he does so here as an individual sinner, not as *Kreatur*. There is a judge and law, not arbitrary and unfathomable winds of destiny. The realization that punishment is meted out to the sinner for breaking that law, rather than indiscriminately to all, only confirms the fact of his individuality. For Günther, time does not imply *Vergänglichkeit* as such; rather it is a possession which, though limited, he can spend in a way impossible for Gryphius. At some point in life, there is a "too late"; for Gryphius, to whom life is simply a steady progress toward death from the very moment of birth, such a turning point would be inconceivable.

Such a new view of the self, interwoven with a new sense of time, develops further as the eighteenth century continues. Zinzendorf expresses the position more clearly and powerfully in "Eitelkeit" ("Vanity"):

Verdammte Eitelkeit, Betrügrin meiner Jahre,
Der ich bereits dahin, ich weiß nicht wohin, fahre!
Erkenne ich dein Gift, des Hofes Sclaverei,
Und sehe, wie ich mir selbst feind geworden sei?

Ich sehe, daß ich nur die Blüte meiner Tage
Gar jämmerlich versäumt, und leg ich auf die Wage,
Was für den Leib getan, und für der Seele Heil,
So hatte jener Lust, und diese Langeweil.

13. *Deutsche Barocklyrik*, ed. Martin Sommerfeld (Berlin, 1934), p. 33.

Halt ein, verwegner Lauf vertriebner Zeit und Stunden!
Ich habe in Zeiten noch den Weg zurückgefunden!
Ich eile und wohin? Bishero wußt ichs nicht;

Doch jetzo eile ich von Finsternis zum Licht,
Zum Hirten, der mich ruft, zu Salems ewgem Hügel;
Bedrängte Seele, laß der Regung Zaum und Zügel!

(Accursed vanity, deceiver of my years,
I who have already travelled, although I know not where!
Shall I recognize your venom, the slavery of the court,
And see how I've become my own worst enemy?

I see how the spring and summer of my life
Have gone to seed so wretchedly, and if I take in balance
What I've done for my body and for my soul's salvation,
The former had the pleasure, the latter only boredom.

Halt, foolhardy course of banished time and hours,
In time still I have found the road that leads me back!
I hurry—and whereto? Til now I did not know;

But now I hasten from the darkness toward the light,
To the shepherd, who summons me, to th' eternal hill of Salem;
O my oppressed soul, let loose the bridle of your feelings!)[14]

In call and echo, question and answer, in the several variations of
the concepts of time and motion, the sonnet drives us along with a
necessity comparable to that found in Gryphius. The press, however, is no longer that of time itself, but is the intense haste of a
man moving toward a clearly defined goal. The individual rules
time, casts it at will into one or the other pan of the scales. It is
really not "time," however, but "times"—years, days, hours. Indeed,
we can almost speak of two "times," a lost, wasted time, which has
gone its reckless way, and a second which seems to be moving in
another direction, or which at any rate has a definite goal. In this
world man is the center of force. Standing at the "helm" himself,
he can steer and direct time—and his own life—so long as he knows
the right direction. Unlike the "Ich" of Gryphius' "Abend," the
speaker does not need to be torn by force from the darkness, but
hurries out of it and into the light under his own power. He does
not lose his identity, but, becoming "his own enemy," temporarily

14. *Deutsche Barocklyrik*, pp. 34–35.

mistakes his best interests. He does not need to search for the self, but only for the right "way." Although intense motion is the essence of both sonnets, with Gryphius the movement comes from outside, carrying the passive individual along directly to destruction. In the Zinzendorf poem, the motive force in life comes from within the individual, who is ultimately in control and must choose his path.

The growing self-confidence expressed by Zinzendorf depends partly on a belief in a world governed by universally valid Divine law rather than a kind of spiritualized imperial whim, which Gryphius' poetry tends to reflect. The transition, however, begins already with Günther and the slowly shifting view of the role and significance of the individual. It will culminate in the eighteenth century when man, again the center of the universe, as he was before in the Renaissance, finds himself and security as a necessary link in the great chain of being, that panacea-like concept of the Enlightenment which Pope will call upon in his "Essay on Man" to explain or explain away all human suffering with the words "whatever is, is right." If Zinzendorf rides in any vessel, it is more likely to be a pounding chariot with firm land under its wheels than a ship on the treacherous seas. When the poet does take to the sea again in the later eighteenth century, we should rather expect to find the individual at the helm of the ship, directing its course and sure of his goal, with that firm confidence in his ability to guide and take responsibility for his destiny that Goethe indicates in "Seefahrt" ("Sea Voyage"):

> Doch er stehet männlich an dem Steuer:
> Mit dem Schiffe spielen Wind und Wellen,
> Wind und Wellen nicht mit seinem Herzen.
> Herrschend blickt er auf die grimme Tiefe
> Und vertrauet, scheiternd oder landend
> Seinen Göttern.

> (But he stands there steadfast at the helm:
> Wind and rushing waves toy with the ship,
> No wind nor waves can so toy with his heart.
> In full control he glances at the threat'ning deep
> And, should he wreck or safely land, entrusts his soul
> Unto his God.)[15]

15. *Goethes Werke,* ed. Erich Trunz, vol. 1 (Hamburg, 1948), p. 50.

# PART II

## The Biblical Word
## as the Poetic Word

# 6

## Auff den Sontag
## deß Sünden vergebenden Trösters

To be judged consistently one of the outstanding poets of
seventeenth-century Germany is to be placed in the distressingly
ambiguous position of being considered one of the best of a group
of poets whose poetry as poetry seems in many respects to have
very little to say to the modern reader. For by and large we have
come to expect, rightly or wrongly, little that is new, appealing, or,
to our perhaps jaded sensibilities, truly exciting in the Neoclassi-
cism of an Opitz or the swollen phrases and often oddly distorted
metaphors and conceits of the later seventeenth-century poets. The
tenor and thrust of the commentaries made by Baroque scholars
over the years, stressing primarily the derivative and normative aspects of this poetry, is somehow not surprising. Nor is it surprising
that Baroque scholarship contains few detailed studies of individual
poems, for it is a poetry which seems to lend itself much more
readily to generalizations based on a more cursory reading of large
numbers than to the incisive analysis of single examples. And certainly it is probably fair to say that this is not a poetry that bears
frequent re-reading for the flashes of new insight or the reward of
hitherto unremarked beauty to be gleaned from each new perusal.
Its main significance has often seemed to be historical, consisting

less of what it *is* as poetry than of what its creators attempted to
bring with it from elsewhere to a language which had not yet developed an awareness of its own capacity for poetic expression.
Ironically, what this poetry ultimately did bring proved to be at
one and the same time its own weakness and the necessary funda-
ment for the future greatness of German literature. For its essential
contribution was not volume upon volume of imitations, some successful, some not, of Petrarch and Ronsard and the Latin poets of
the Middle Ages, but rather an abstract quality whose concrete
precipitate informs the poetry of the entire age—a pervasive sense
of stability and order. Little wonder that, having taken as the ideal
a post-Goethean poetry whose very existence depends upon an immensely rich personal involvement and which develops its own
laws and its own unity from within itself, it has taken so long to
learn how even to begin to come to terms with the lyric of the
Baroque. In a poetry so concerned with the establishment of form
and the perfection of technique, and necessarily so well-ordered by
external norms, there could be little room for the uniquely personal
and individual, for *das Einmalige,* which is by its very nature spontaneous and iconoclastic and cannot be submitted to such external
governing regulations and controls.

The main body of Gryphius criticism since Manheimer's diligent study early in this century appears to place his poetry too
squarely into this traditional scheme. Presented as a child of his
age, he emerges as a conformist who does not even revise his
poems, but rather painstakingly and mechanically corrects his
minor transgressions against the laws of rhetoric and the prevailing
theories of poetics, a poet who is more than willing to yield to convention, even when such submission could only adversely affect
the quality of his poetry. And nowhere is this rigidity in the critical
posture of Gryphius scholarship more apparent than in the treatment of his two cycles of *Sonn-und Feiertagssonette,* which has
focused on the assumed fact of the poet's orthodoxy in both literary
and religious matters. Gryphius' Protestantism and the Bible, which
served as a source for his religious lyrics, represent, after all, yet another norm. Since he wrote *geistliche Lieder* in an already well-
established tradition of religious lyric, for example, and because of
his familiarity with and admiration for the works of such orthodox
Protestant hymnists as Johann Heermann, there has been a tendency to treat the *Sonn-und Feiertagssonette* also like the numerous

religious songs by other Protestant writers prior to and during the
generation in which Gryphius lived. Consequently, these two books
of sonnets have regularly been considered to be further examples
of an orthodox, conforming, conventional, and thus completely un-
surprising *Perikopendichtung*. At least in part as a result of this
view, the sonnets, which number together one hundred poems,
have largely been neglected as objects of critical interpretation and
analysis. As has already been pointed out above, however, in the
discussion of "Es ist alles eitell," too one-sided a reliance on a poet's
acceptance of and strict adherence to the imposed literary traditions of his day—and this whether it be Gryphius or Goethe who is
to be considered—with the accompanying neglect of poet and
poem as individual entities, inevitably leads to deficiencies in interpretation. In Gryphius' case, more often than not, such an atti-
tude has resulted in errors of omission, for the critic has succumbed
much too easily to the temptation of disregarding or simply failing
to look for much more than superficial matters. Just as it seems im-
proper to approach Gryphius too dogmatically as a child of his age,
so too, a judgment of his religious poetry resting on the assumption
that its author is merely a conforming child of his church would
seem invalid. Although these first two books of sonnets are certainly uneven in quality, or perhaps just because of that, they
cannot be classified together as indiscriminately as has been done
in the past.

   The consequences can be seen already in Manheimer's discussion of the poems. He begins by stating that the most important
convention for Gryphius was the religious convention, and then
continues: "Zwar lag ihm in Stücken, die sich an Bibeltexte anlehn-
ten, wenig daran, ob sie sich von dem Wortlaut der Lutherschen
Übersetzung entfernten oder sich ihm wieder näherten; er faßte
diese Art Gedichte als Variationen auf, bei denen es nicht darauf
ankam, ob das variierte Bibelmotiv mehr oder weniger deutlich zu
erkennen war. Dagegen achtete er ziemlich aufmerksam darauf,
daß gewisse Begriffe und Worte, an denen sich orthodoxe Beur-
teiler hätten stoßen können, nicht wiederkehrten." ("Indeed, in
those poems which were modelled after biblical texts, he was little
concerned with whether they departed greatly from the wording
of the Lutheran translation or approached it closely; he considered
poems of this type as variations in which it was not a question of
whether the varied biblical motif could be recognized more or less

easily. On the other hand, he was quite careful to make certain
that certain concepts and words which orthodox critics could have
taken amiss did not re-appear.")[1] Such a conclusion is an oversimplification. It seems much more likely that Gryphius is indeed concerned with the degree of dependence upon the biblical texts
which his sonnets exhibit, though in a manner quite different from
that of a Plauen or a Heermann. He is, for example, not a hymnist,
a fact which seems to play no role in Manheimer's evaluations, but
which obviously must be considered in any serious comment on the
poems. Manheimer's conclusions notwithstanding, the sonnets are
more than simply variations on the respective scriptural texts, and
both their correspondence to and their deviations from the biblical
sources must be examined much more carefully before any satisfactory conclusions can be drawn about them. In addition, a consideration of the uses to which Gryphius puts the biblical material
at his disposal, together with some reflection on the purpose of
these poems, is indispensable. Similarly, while it is true that the
*Sonn-und Feiertagssonette* as a whole show the influence, to greater
and lesser degrees, of several earlier writers, we cannot, in interpretation and evaluation, dwell too long on alleged similarities between the verse of Gryphius and that of Heermann or Plauen, as
Manheimer does, without concerning ourselves to any great extent with the dissimilarities. Here, too, Manheimer in his discussions
stays close to the formal aspects of the poetry and is very often too
general in his comments. To state that "Plauens häufigste Stilmittel
sind die Anapher und die Klangmalerei. Grade darin hat er auf
Gryphius gewirkt" ("Plauen's most frequent stylistic characteristics
are anapher and onomatopoeia. Precisely in these devices he influenced Gryphius"),[2] is to tell us really very little about the influence of the one poet upon the other, particularly in an age when
such rhetorical devices are not only common property and a part
of the background of every poet, but are also constantly emphasized by most authors. Any actual "influence" of one poet upon another does not descend in such a simple and direct line, and when
it can be proven, it must certainly extend beyond and be clearly
visible in more than this sort of external superficiality. Similarly,
rhyme-echoes or even correspondences in rhyme between individual poems of Heermann and Gryphius based upon the same chapters of the Bible, while offering evidence of Gryphius' close fa-

1. Manheimer, pp. 104–5.        2. Manheimer, p. 132.

miliarity with Heermann's *Lieder,* do not in themselves contribute much to a convincing picture of a strong, lasting, or significant influence. This is especially so when such characteristics are presented as they are by Manheimer, with no discussion of similarities in *content* between the poems cited. It is precisely such differences in content and purpose, both as they exist between Gryphius and his biblical sources and between Gryphius and other poets utilizing the same sources, that will be discussed in this section.

Such "Sunday and Holiday" poems and church songs, cycles of poems based on the corresponding biblical text for each Sunday and holiday of the church year and following the church calendar, were a popular means of transmitting the ideas of the Scriptures to the layman. When set to music, as they almost invariably were, they also offered a method of combatting the increasing popularity of secular songs. Gryphius, however, remains one of the few German poets to fashion these religious poems as sonnets, and he is also one of the earliest to do so. Manheimer mentions Werder (1631) as the first German poet to use the sonnet in this manner as a vehicle for biblical material, followed then by Plauen, Gryphius, and Fleming. Gryphius' employment of such a distinctly literary form as the sonnet, and a stringent and demanding one at that, in which he clearly writes his best poetry and feels himself to be most at home—this, together with the fact that the sonnets were apparently at no time intended by the author to be set to music for use inside or outside the church, constitutes already on external grounds no small difference between them and the traditional *Sonn- und Feiertags Lieder.* The poetry of Gryphius or of Paul Fleming belongs to a new type of religious lyric just then developing alongside of and partly out of the *Kirchenlied.* Three of the Sunday sonnets will be considered in this and the next two chapters, and a group of several other religious sonnets in the concluding chapter, in an attempt to determine more clearly just what kind of poetry this was in Gryphius' case. The discussions are conducted in the belief that in these religious lyrics, as well as in the secular sonnets, it is the poet Gryphius, rather than the orthodox Protestant, who comes to the fore. The clearest evidence of this dominance of the poet can be seen in a subtlety and a care in the use of language not usually attributed to these two cycles. These in turn can stem only from the poet's keen awareness both of the poetic form itself and of the role of the poet, both of which are always in his mind.

By way of introduction, the sonnet "Auff den Sontag deß Sünden vergebenden Trösters" affords an example of the techniques
used by Gryphius in transforming the biblical into the poetic word.
Matthew 9, on which the sonnet is based, deals with a series of
miracles performed by Jesus, all the episodes of which, except the
first, that of the paralytic, are concerned solely with the miraculous
healing of physical illness. Gryphius' sonnet, however, makes use of
only this first segment comprising the first six verses of the chapter,
in which the paralytic's sins are first forgiven and then, to satisfy
the skeptical scribes, his infirmity is healed:

1. DA trat er in das Schiff, vnd fuhr wider herüber, vnd kam
   in seine Stadt.
2. Vnd sihe, da brachten sie zu jm einen Gichtbrüchigen, der
   lag auff einem bette. Da nu Jhesus jren Glauben sahe, sprach
   er zu dem Gichtbrüchigen, Sey getrost, mein Son, deine
   sünde sind dir vergeben.
3. VNd sihe, etliche vnter den Schrifftgelerten, sprachen bey
   sich selbs, Dieser lestert Gott.
4. Da aber Jhesus jre gedancken sahe, sprach er, Warumb
   denckt jr so arges in ewren hertzen?
5. Welchs ist leichter zu sagen? dir sind deine sünde vergeben?
   Oder zu sagen, stehe auff vnd wandele?
6. Auff das jr aber wisset, das des menschen Son macht habe
   auff Erden, die sünde zu vergeben, sprach er zu dem Gichtbrüchigen, Stehe auff, heb dein bette auff, vnd gehe heim.
7. Vnd er stund auff, vnd gieng heim.[3]

The Gryphius sonnet follows:

Auff den Sontag deß Sünden vergebenden Trösters / oder
XIX. Sontag nach dem Fest der H. Dreyeinigkeit. Math. 9.

(On the Sunday of the Consoler who Forgives Our Sins /
or Nineteenth Sunday after the Festival of the Holy
Trinity. Matthew 9.)

Dünckts iemand frembde, daß ich in der Angst verschwinde?
Daß theurer Mittel-fleiß und werther Kräuter Macht /

---

3. All extended biblical citations are from *D. Martin Luthers Werke,*
vols. 6, 11, *Die Deutsche Bibel,* kritische Gesamtausgabe, ed. Hans Volz (reprint of 1883 edition; Weimar, 1962).

Daß weiser Aertzte Kunst mir noch nicht wieder bracht,
Was Sucht und Angst verzehrt? Die grimme Pein die Sünde /
Greifft mich von innen an. Mein Heiland ich befinde
    Daß alles nur umbsonst nach dem ein Krancker tracht,
    Weil diese Gifft noch wehr't. Kom' eh' ich gantz
                                  [verschmacht,
O Sünden tilger komm / komm eilendts und entbinde
    Mein fest verstricktes Hertz / das so voll Boßsheit steckt /
    Da rohe Sicherheit / Seuch über Seuchen heckt.
Sprich: Sey getrost mein Kind! Ich habe dir vergeben,
    Wormit du mich erzürnt: Ich habe deine Noth
    Gewendet: ja dein Creutz geendet; und den Tod
Verschlungen / daß du magst unendlich für mir leben.
                                (*Werke* 1: 217)


(Does it seem strange to anyone that I am wasting away
                                  [from fear?
That neither expensive medicines, nor the power of valued
                                  [herbs,
Nor the arts of the wisest doctors can help me regain my
                                  [health,
Consumed by corruption and fear? That grim torment, sin,
Attacks me from within. My Saviour, I must own
That every antidote a sick man tries is futile,
The while this poison works. Come, else I pass away,
Redeemer of my sins, come quickly and set free
My heart so tightly bound, so full of wickedness,
Where proud self-confidence breeds sickness upon sickness.
Speak: I bring comfort, my child, I have forgiven you
That which caused my ire: your misery I have
Transformed, the very cross you bore cast off, and death
Devoured, that you may live with me eternally.)


It is interesting to recognize the speaker of these lines. At first
glance, the introductory quartet might be that of any of a number
of poems written by Gryphius on physical illness and deterioration
of the body and its powers. The sonnet "Thränen in schwerer
kranckheit" ("Tears While Sorely Ill"), for example, comes to mind:

Mir ist ich weis nicht wie / ich seufftze für undt für.
    Ich weine tag undt nacht / ich sitz in tausend schmertzen;
    Undt tausendt fürcht ich noch / die krafft in meinem hertzen

Verschwindt / der geist verschmacht / die hände sincken
[mir.

(*Werke* 1: 59)

(I am—I know not how, I sigh for hours on end,
I weep all day and night, life is a thousand torments,
And a thousand more I fear yet. The strength within my heart
Dissolves, my spirit pines, my hands sink helplessly.)

Yet our knowledge of the biblical passage concerned would seem
to indicate that the speaker is in fact the paralytic himself, and
that, as in Matthew, there is a question here both of the healing of
physical affliction and forgiveness of sin, facts apparently borne out
by the remainder of the sonnet. It would then appear that the poet,
having put himself in the place of the paralytic, who does not
speak in the Scriptures at all, now gives us an expression of what
the latter's thoughts might have been, in the form of a sonnet.
However, as will be indicated in the treatment of the poem on the
following pages, the relationship of the speaker in the poem to the
paralytic in the Bible is more complex, as is the role played by physical illness.

Interestingly, in the original version of the sonnet, line one
read as follows: "Dünckts iemandt frembt, daß ich in *kranckheit*
so verschwinde" (italics mine). The change in all editions after the
first from "Kranckheit" to "Angst" is a significant one in view of the
lines that follow, for even here in the very first line of his poem
Gryphius has begun a process which is to culminate with the final
lines of the sonnet by which the theme of the poem is removed
from the realm of the physical. At the same time, he has internal-
ized what is in the biblical account an external matter.[4] The meaning of the remainder of the first quartet must immediately become
at least ambiguous when it is realized that it is fear and not physical affliction or death that is the threatening force here. The result
is a typically Gryphian illusion, created by the application of the
poetic word to the original biblical word. For, while the first three
and one-half lines of the sonnet seem to paraphrase the Scriptures
by presenting the paralytic's thoughts, there has in fact been a shift

4. For a valuable study of the significance to Gryphius of *Angst*, see
Isabella Rüttenauer's "Die Angst des Menschen in der Lyrik des Andreas
Gryphius," in *Aus der Welt des Barock* (Stuttgart, 1957), pp. 36–55. Miss
Rüttenauer, however, makes no mention of the interesting occurrence of the
word in the revision of this poem.

in emphasis from the physical to the spiritual. While the physical and the spiritual in Matthew run parallel to each other in the two episodes of forgiveness of sins and the miraculous cure, in the sonnet, the physical—stated only in terms of the inadequacy of the remedies available—serves only to heighten the dominance of the spiritual ills of the speaker. In the best tradition of Gryphius and the Baroque, the two elements are here juxtaposed antithetically. While the possibility still exists that the poet simply describes a physical ailment in the first four lines, it is no longer necessary, once the motif of *Angst* is established in the sonnet, to consider the physical at all. Rather, the disorder elaborated in lines two and three is an internal state of mind, fear, against which external natural and man-made remedies can have no effect. Again in line four an interesting revision should be noted, the substitution of "Sucht" for "schmerz" in all editions after the Leyden printing of 1639. It is a change which supports the progressive movement in the poem away from the idea of the external and purely physical and toward the internal mental and spiritual suffering caused by man's ultimately necessary confrontation with sin. Grimm's *Wörterbuch* cites the first four lines of this poem in its discussion of the historical development of the meaning of the word "Sucht." Gryphius' use here, according to this article, is an example of an extension of the original meaning of *Sucht*, i.e., any specific physical illness, *Kranckheit*. The meaning is, however, still firmly rooted in the realm of the physical: "von der basis 1 b aus tritt gelegentlich eine erweiterung des bedeutungsraumes ein, indem der bezug auf concrete krankheitsbilder hinter dem allgemeinen vorstellungsinhalt körperlichen übelfindens zurücktritt, das sachwort sich einer zustandsbezeichnung nähert, *sucht* rückt dann in die stelle eines negativen gegenbegriffes zu *gesundheit* ein und umschreibt den zustand des krankseins schlechthin . . ." ("proceeding from the basis 1b, an expansion of meaning takes place, in that the reference to concrete images of illness retreats behind the general idea of physical malaise, and the word that previously designated a specific thing now approaches in meaning a designation of a condition. "Sucht" then assumes the position of a negative contrary to "Gesundheit" and describes the condition of being ill in general . . ."). Confirmation of the reference of "Sucht" to physical ailment is seen clearly in the example given for its usage in this sense directly before the passage from Gryphius is cited in this subdivision of the article: "als auch die sucht und krankheit desz menschlichen verweszlichen leibs im wenigsten nichts gegen der fälschung und verlust der aller kostbarlichsten seelen zu schätzen GUARINONI *grewel der verwüstung* (1610)" ("as is also true that illness or sickness of the mortal, insubstantial body is not at all to be valued in comparison to the falsification and the loss of the most valuable souls, GUARINONI *horrors of devastation* [1610]"). (*DWB* 10, no. 4: 865). Yet such an assumption that the meaning of "Sucht" in the Gryphius poem refers unambiguously to the physical state of the speaker cannot be accepted when the context is considered and when more far-reaching meaning changes of this word, which are discussed later in the same article in the *DWB*, are noted. At the very beginning of this section, in a general discussion of the overall semantic change which the word underwent throughout the centuries, it is stated that *Sucht,* in its original meaning of physical illness (*körperliche Krankheit*), was much more widely used than any of its synonyms until the sixteenth century, but that since that time its use in this meaning has had to be strengthened and supported by the addition of qualifying synonyms. The synonym most frequently used from this period on seems to have been *Krankheit.* Of importance is the fact that precisely in the seventeenth century, according to Grimm, the decisive reversal in meaning, "der entscheidende Rückzug," takes place. By the middle of the eighteenth century *Sucht* is generally outmoded in the written language as a designation for sickness, and by the nineteenth century it has disappeared except regionally. *Sucht,* Grimm goes on to mention, existed also in the meaning of *sittliche, seelische, geistige Krankheit* (moral, spiritual illness, illness of the soul)—and more specifically, within this frame of reference, the word describes "den zustand der sündhaftigkeit, dem der mensch durch handlungen oder einflüsse anheimfällt, oder auch die erbsünde als stigma alles kreatürlichen" ("the condition of a state of sin, which attacks man through actions or influences, or also original sin, as the stigma of all this earth") ( *DWB*, pp. 860, 885). Ringwaldt, with whose *geistliche Lieder* Gryphius was acquainted, and Angelus Silesius are quoted in Grimm as examples of the users of the word with this meaning. It is clear that the latter use of *Sucht* was current at the time of the writing of this sonnet. The substitution, then, of "Sucht" for "schmerz" is not that of a general word for a specific; rather, two different realms of human existence are concerned here: on the one hand, the purely physical;

on the other, the inner, the spiritual. In the first three and one-half
lines of the original version the idea of physical disorder and approaching physical death is explicit; the revision, which still could
be taken to imply the physical, introduces also, however, in a kind
of counter-point and by means of a sensitive use of language, the
other pole of the great antithesis—the inner spiritual state, as it is
inescapably affected by sin. This theme dominates the remainder
of the poem, which begins now to look less and less like those sonnets purporting to describe the poet's various physical complaints.

It is actually only with the second quartet that the cause of
the suffering and fears of the first four lines is made clear. With the
use of the word "Pein" in the second half of line four, a substitution
for "Sucht" in the earliest version, which now cannot be repeated,
the transition from external, physical pain to internal, mental suffering is clearly marked. The word has a three-fold meaning, and
no one of its parts can be ignored. In addition to the concept of
physical agony, there is, by virtue of its origin, the religious-
dogmatic connotation of the torments of hell attached to it, as well
as the idea of internal mental anguish in anticipation thereof. These
overtones lead directly to the remainder of line four and the first
half of line five, where we have finally arrived at the heart of the
matter: the transition from the physical is here completed, and we
are for the first time unequivocally in the realm of sin and spiritual
torment. It can be no accident that just at this point the transition
in meaning is paralleled in form by an enjambement that links the
first quartet with the second and thereby leads directly from the
physical to the spiritual. The image of the sick man is repeated in
the second quartet, but there is no doubt now that "ein Krancker"
of line six and "Gifft" of line seven are metaphors, that the illness is
not physical, and that the fear is not of death, but of what must
follow it. Similarly, if "Seuchen" of line ten is reminiscent of "Sucht"
of line four, the malady of the quartet is, nevertheless, spiritual
and internal by nature, and never again after this point is there a
possible allusion to simply physical death. "Creutz" of line thirteen
is sin, and even if "den Tod" of the same line *were* taken to denote
physical death, it would be the cessation of life on earth seen not of
itself but as a result of man's sin.

A word must be said here of the rhythm and meter of the
poem, which reveal once again Gryphius' sensitivity to the effective use of both and offer some evidence of how he was able to re-

main within the alexandrine and yet not be fettered by it. In the best of Gryphius' sonnets, the formal meter never dominates, but rather, while all the metrical requirements of the sonnet form are fulfilled, it is the rhythm that is more striking. Gryphius is well aware of the danger of stagnation and of outright boredom that can result from the unrelieved regularity of the alexandrine's sequence of stressed and unstressed syllables. There is ample evidence that Gryphius made conscious efforts to avoid the problem by creating and stressing rhythmic patterns which he employed as functional elements of his poems to help subordinate the technically control-ling meter, which here is more apt to become a merely abstract convention than elsewhere in the Baroque. As had been noted above, for example, in "Es ist alles eitell" a repeated rhythmic con-figuration works to unify and bind the sonnet. An examination of the metrical and rhythmic structure of "Auff den Sontag deß Sün-den vergebenden Trösters" discloses that, with the clear exception of line one and the last two and one-half lines, Gryphius follows quite closely the normal alexandrine, with no striking rhythms to lessen its prominence. Lines two through eleven consist almost ex-clusively of sequences of stressed and unstressed syllables in regu-lar alternation. The division of each line into two equal halves of three feet each is marked by the caesura, as well as by the fact that both the caesura and the end of the line ordinarily coincide with the end of a syntactical unit or a unit of thought. Even with the enjambement at the end of line four, the feminine final syllable of line four plus the use of "Sünde" as an appositive permit an actual, if slight pause at the conclusion of line four. At the end of line eight, the unstressed final syllable likewise works against the enjambement, despite the separation at this point of the verb and its direct object. The colon usually coincides here with the three-foot half-line, and there is never tension or conflict between rhythm and meter. There is, however, a gradual loosening of the pattern as the sonnet proceeds into the second quartet, such that the nat-ural rhythm begins to emerge as an independent element not to be limited by the formal meter. Thus, while lines two through four begin with the easily unstressed subordinating conjunction "Daß" and the relative pronoun "Was," after the enjambement at the end of line four, line five begins strongly with the verb "Greifft," which must take at least a secondary stress, although according to the meter it should remain unstressed. In the same line there is a strong second caesura after "Heiland," while the preceding "Mein" cannot remain completely unstressed. Again in line six the first syllable after the caesura, the imperative "Kom'," is much too strong to remain without stress. But this increase in the intensity of the rhythm is a gradual process which culminates only in the second tercet, where the poem as a whole reaches its climax.

Much more than a metrically correct line is required for the last two and one-half verses of the sonnet, which close the poem with a strong surge of optimistic anticipation. The emotional climax reached in the last tercet is both reflected in and aided by the rhythm of the lines. A complex of poetic and rhetorical devices helps to create, from the middle of line twelve, a constantly rising inflection which reaches its peak just before the early caesura in line fourteen and then falls off gently until the end of the poem. From the caesura after the third foot of line twelve, the reader is forced to hurry along until the postponed climax in line fourteen because of the enjambements at the end of lines twelve and thirteen, coupled with the early caesura of thirteen, which results in an extremely long colon following it. The necessity of reading on without pause at the ends of lines twelve and thirteen because of the separation of the auxiliary verb from its participle is strengthened by the masculine ending of each of these lines, for in both cases the sequence of iambs thus remains unbroken by an extra unstressed syllable. While the extended colon, beginning with the caesura in line twelve, ends with the caesura of line thirteen, the pitch continues to rise until the end of the very long colon at the caesura of fourteen. The force of these lines and the extension of the rising inflection which contributes so much to that force are brought about most of all by the syntactical pattern evolved and the resulting tension of the lines. To follow this development it will be necessary to return to line eleven and the first use of the syntactical combination of "habe" plus the past participle. While the main stress falls on the participle, the end of the line is both the end of the clause and of the main thought of the sentence, so that the inflection drops with the subordinate clause that begins line twelve. With the repetition of this pattern in lines twelve and thirteen, however—and the very repetition serves to strengthen the lines— the distance between the auxiliary verb and its participle, which does not now appear until the beginning of the next line, thirteen, and thus is also stressed by its position, has been increased. The

omission then in line thirteen of the auxiliary, which is understood
with the following two participles, would normally have caused a
drop in inflection, but combines with the elements noted above to
maintain the pitch until "Verschlungen" of line fourteen. The colon
here has gradually been expanded:

> . . . Ich habe dir vergeben,
> . . . Ich habe deine Noth
> Gewendet: ja dein Creutz geendet; und den Tod
> Verschlungen. . . .

The net result of these factors is a group of dynamic lines which
move forward forcefully until the final completion of the thought
of this one extended main clause and, at the same time, a relaxation of the tension at the caesura of fourteen. In this tercet the
rhythm prevails over the formal meter, although the latter remains
intact and breaks through, for the moment, the limits imposed by
the sonnet form. The tension that evolves is further aided by the
internal rhyme "Gewendet"/"geendet" of line thirteen. This internal
rhyme, together with the irregularly placed caesuras, the
lengthened cola of lines twelve through fourteen, and the enjambements in twelve and thirteen, helps to de-emphasize the normal
end-rhyme of lines twelve and thirteen. All of the above-mentioned
characteristics of these lines are deviations, however slight, from a
pattern, either that created by the author in this poem, or that of
the sonnet form itself. These deviations, by virtue of their non-
conformity, help to shift the attention of the reader away from that
pattern. Such a tension, or balance, between an established pattern
and variations upon it, contributes greatly to the unique power of
effective poetry.

The sonnet ends with the calm of line fourteen, with a gentle-
ness brought about by the finally dropping inflection, and a softness
produced by a sensitive combination of assonance and an unusual
number of liquids and nasals—there is only one voiceless stop in
the entire line—which produce generally soft combinations of
vowels and consonants. If line one, which is at once statement,
question, and exclamation, ends on a note of imminent death, the
poem runs full cycle and ends naturally in line fourteen with the
hope of life, though on another, higher level. This contrast is
brought to the reader not only by the content of the verses, but

also by the form of the two lines. Line one is the only line of the sonnet aside from the lines of the second tercet that has its one caesura before the third foot and, as a result, a comparatively long colon in its second half. While it is not exactly parallel to line fourteen in its form, rhythmic similarities are clearly present between the two lines.

For the reader who is familiar with the Bible, as Gryphius' seventeenth-century readers certainly were to a far greater extent than we, the two aspects of the story of Matthew 9, the curing of the paralytic's physical ailment and the forgiveness of his sins by Jesus, come to mind as the poem is read. But, as elsewhere within these two sonnet cycles on the Sundays and holidays, while Gryphius establishes from the first a clear connection between the biblical source and his poem, he goes beyond the mere repetition of scriptural narrative embellished by the formal trappings of poetry. He does not merely transpose matter already furnished into the form of lyric by adding rhyme and the required meter, but transforms material already given. Striking in the sonnet is the gradual fading away of all concern with what is external and superficial, physical life and death—indeed, as has been pointed out above, the physical is not a serious issue at all. So important in the sonnet is the internal state of the narrator and the question of spiritual life that in the first line the physical cause of his condition has been removed. The sonnet thereafter concerns itself only with another, a spiritual life and death, and the internal fears about the state of the soul. Fear appears as the illness of man, and we should expect no less from Gryphius.

The general tenor of the poem is completely different from that of the supporting Bible passage. Its anguished plea for redemption, made in fear, is not in harmony with the biblical "cure," which takes place only because of the calm, silent, unquestioning faith of the paralytic. The version in the Scriptures, furthermore, remains impersonal so far as the paralytic is concerned, the story centering rather on Jesus and his powers, and it remains only one of several similar accounts. Gryphius, however, shifts the emphasis to the position of the individual before God, his inner feelings and attitudes, his despair, and his hope. Thus, only the "afflicted" speaks in the poem, which is not so much didactic, as descriptive. There is no warning, no admonition, no preacher making use of the biblical word and indicating how it is to be applied, no explanation of how one is to live his life or attain the eternal. Nor is this a simple statement of the power and the mercy of the Divine, as it is in the Bible, as true today as it was then. Rather, it is a troubled plea that what was so then may be true today, still or again, and that the mercy of Jesus be extended to all. For who is the speaker of the poem who quotes Jesus in line eleven, "Sprich: Sey getrost mein Kind! Ich habe dir vergeben," if not the poet himself, representing each individual man, who must himself eventually face the same fears and hopes? It is the poet who asks that the same mercy shown once to the paralytic now be granted to him and to all like him. Gryphius here adapts the words of the Scriptures to a peculiarly Lutheran view of salvation—man stands alone before God in sin, passively awaiting the action of the Divine; only in Divine action, and in nothing that man can do himself, lies his salvation. What is stated in Matthew with certainty as fact remains in the sonnet in the realm of anticipation and hope.

# 7

## Auf den sontag
## des versuchten sohnes Gottes

In the previous chapter an attempt was made to show that in his sonnets based on the gospels Gryphius does more than simply paraphrase the Scriptures, that with his refashioning of the biblical word something deeply personal is added. The transformation of biblical statement as evidenced in the sonnet "Auf den Sonntag deß Sünden vergebenden Trösters" should not be considered as merely an isolated case. On the contrary, a similar process by which the revealed word of God becomes the poetic word can be observed in many of the sonnets of these two groups, as the discussion of two further poems will attempt to show. A reading of the sonnet "Auf den sontag des versuchten sohnes Gottes" reveals here, too, marked differences from the biblical text on which it is based. The metamorphosis of the biblical word proceeds just as subtly, but in its own fashion. Given below are those verses of Matthew 4 which serve as the sonnet's source and the poem itself:

1. DA ward Jhesus vom Geist in die Wüsten gefürt, Auff das er von dem Teuffel versucht würde.
2. Vnd da er vierzig tag und vierzig nacht gefastet hatte, hungert jn.

3. Vnd der Versucher trat zu jm, vnd sprach, Bistu Gottes son, so sprich, das diese stein brot werden.

4. Vnd er antwortet, vnd sprach, Es stehet geschrieben, Der Mensch lebet nicht vom Brot alleine, Sondern von einem jglichen wort, das durch den mund Gottes gehet.

5. DA füret jn der Teufel mit sich, in die heilige Stad, vnd stellet jn auff die zinnen des Tempels,

6. vnd sprach zu jhm, Bistu Gottes son, so las dich hinab, Denn es stehet geschrieben, Er wird seinen Engeln vber dir befelh thun, Vnd sie werden dich auff den henden tragen, Auff das du deinen fuss nicht an einen stein stössest.

7. Da sprach Jhesus zu jm, Widerumb stehet auch geschrieben, Du solt Gott deinen HERRN nicht versuchen.

8. WJderumb füret jn der Teufel mit sich, auff einen seer hohen Berg, vnd zeiget jm alle Reich der Welt, vnd jre Herrligkeit,

9. Vnd sprach zu jm, Das alles wil ich dir geben, So du niderfellest, vnd mich anbetest.

10. Da sprach Jhesus zu jm, Heb dich weg von mir Satan, Denn es stehet geschrieben, Du solt anbeten Gott deinen HERRN, vnd jm allein dienen.

11. DA verlies jn der Teufel, Vnd sihe, da tratten die Engel zu jm vnd dieneten jm.


Auf den sontag des versuchten sohnes Gottes, oder
Invocavit, Matth. 4.
(On the Sunday of the Tempted Son of God, or
Invocavit, Matthew 4)


Weg! weg! hinweg du stoltzer geist! dafern mir schon die
[raue wüsten,
In welcher Gott mich prüfen will, nichts als nur harte steine
[weist,
Wird meine matte seele doch durch dessen kräftig's wort
[gespeist,
Der alles brodt und speise schafft. Dafern du gleich mit
[schlimmen listen
Mich in den abgrund stürtzen willst, wird mich doch dessen
[allmacht fristen,
Der für die seinen treulich sorgt, der in dem weg uns bleiben
[heißt,
Der durch der engel starcken schutz den seinen festen
[beistand leist,

Und nicht von uns versucht will seyn! du wirst doch (glaub
                    ich) keinen christen
Der seinen Jesus treulich meynt, durch tolle herrlichkeit der
                    [welt,
Durch prächtig auffgeschmücktes nichts, durch wollust und
                    [vergänglich geld,
Bewegen, dass er knie und herz, ohnmächtig wunder! vor
                    [dir neige?
Komm an! versuche wie du wilst! Ich wil, weil Jesus für
                    [mich bat,
Der deine gantze macht zustört und dir den kopff zutreten
                    [hat,
Dir erbfeind widerstehen, bis er die ehren-kron mir endlich
                    [zeige.

(Be gone, be gone, thou proud spirit! although to me this
                    [barren wasteland,
In which my God does seek to test me, can offer nought but
                    [stubborn stones,
My weary soul will nonetheless be nourished by the mighty
                    [word
Of Him who creates all our nourishment. Although with evil
                    [cunning
Thou seekst to plunge me to the depths, yet will His
                    [omnipotence save me,
He who tends so faithfully his flock, who bids us keep this
                    [path,
Who, through His angels' firm protection, affords believers
                    [strong support,
And tested by us will not be! Thou willst, I think, convince
                    [no Christian
Whose faith in Jesus is steadfast, by the sumptuous riches
                    [of this world,
Ornately splendid nothingness, or pleasures and ephemeral
                    [fortunes,
To bend both knee and heart, dazzled by temptation, before
                    [thy throne!
Come on! tempt us as thou likest! Because my Jesus prayed
                    [for me,
He who has destroyed thy might and trampled on thy head,
I shall resist thee, enemy, until I finally glimpse the crown
                    [of honor.)[1]

1. Palm, *Werke,* vol. 3, p. 35. The Palm edition of Gryphius' works,
which has "listen" in line four without variant readings, is used here for the

In this sonnet, more clearly than in "Auff den Sontag deß Sünden vergebenden Trösters," the original correspondence between the poem and its thematic antecedent in Matthew falls away, even though the feeling persists that the poem, at least until almost the very end of the octet, is comprised mainly of the only slightly reworded statements of that biblical passage. The close resemblance stems from the fact that the poet not only consistently employs the biblical images of Matthew to express his ideas, but also follows closely the sequence of events in the biblical account for the presentation of his own poetic rendering, which seems to be thematically strikingly similar. Indeed, with the exception of the first half-line of the sonnet, which appears to be misplaced and will be discussed directly, even the order in which the temptations of the Bible occur is retained in the corresponding series of "temptations" in the poem. Whatever liberties the poet has taken with Matthew in the first section of the sonnet have apparently resulted only in an elaboration of that text, and the changes he has undertaken seem not to alter essentially either the intention or the meaning of the original. In fact, in making his apparently slight modifications by addition to or elaboration on his model, Gryphius returns for much of the imagery and phrasing to other sections of the Bible,[2] a technique which can only have the effect of strengthening the sense of linguistic interdependence that already exists between the poetic and the biblical renderings.

Gryphius begins his sonnet with a conspicuous paraphrase of Jesus' reply to Satan after the third temptation. The exclamation is all the more interesting because it represents the only inconsistency of the sonnet in its reproduction of the sequence of biblical events. The reason for this change of order, of however little

text. The information concerning revisions of this line for the various editions of Gryphius' poetry is based on the extensive corrections to Palm's Learsten made by Manheimer, which appeared first in his *Die Lyrik des Andreas Gryphius.* Szyrocki does not list the variant "listen" for E, the 1663 edition.

2. It is, of course, often impossible to indicate with any degree of certainty that any single image or phrase has been taken directly from one specific Bible passage, since most appear in several places in the scriptures. I have not attempted to determine whether any one biblical context in which an image used here by Gryphius also appears might have been of greater significance to him than another. Of immediate importance here is only the fact that Gryphius obviously does go beyond Matthew 4 for expressions which seem to draw the sonnet closer to the biblical word. I list some possible sources without further comment:

consequence it may seem at first glance, soon becomes clear. There can be no doubt that the line is rhetorically effective because of its force. The reader is thrust immediately and directly into the very heart of the situation. But more important is the fact that these words are the only ones among the three replies to Satan which stem directly and originally from Jesus. Jesus' own reaction rather than Gryphius' adaptation of remarks that occur earlier in the Scriptures, these words seem to mark clearly the speaker of this opening line (and thus apparently also of those that follow) as Jesus himself. A pattern is thereby established by the title of the poem and its first half-line which the reader who is familiar with the biblical passage readily accepts and will apply, perhaps unconsciously, to what follows unless given good reason not to do so. And since what follows immediately are two of the three temptations found in Matthew, also presented in direct address and differing only slightly in form and in choice of words from the biblical passage itself, the reader does assume that the speaker of the sonnet and that of its model are one and the same person. This is no more than would be expected from that type of religious lyric which consists basically of a retelling of the passage chosen. But as the sonnet progresses, it becomes clear that no simple one-to-one relationship exists between it and the verses of Matthew. By the beginning of the sestet we find that the use of a paraphrase of Jesus' words in direct address in the first line of the poem serves only to create the pretense that Jesus himself is the "ich" of the sonnet, a fiction which is apparently developed in order to emphasize the close parallelism between the poem and Matthew. In fact, this attempt to emphasize the biblical aspects and, correspondingly, to de-emphasize the poetic individuality and independence of the sonnet, at least in the octave, may have played a role in the revisions Gryphius undertook in this poem. In the revised version, which is the one cited at the beginning of this chapter, the sonnet form has been loosened, perhaps with the intention of drawing

---

3, *matte seele*. Judges 16: 16; Isaiah 1: 5, 40: 28, 31
3–4, 1 Corinthians 10: 3–4; 1 Kings 22: 27; Psalms 80: 6, 42: 4
5, *abgrund*. Apocrypha 9: 1–2; Sirach 21: 11
6, 1 Peter 5: 7
7, *Beistand*. Psalms 60: 13, 108: 13
10, *wollust*. James 4: 1
    *vergänglich geld*. 1 Peter 1: 7
14, James 4: 7; 1 Peter 5: 4; James 1: 12; Apocrypha 2: 10

the reader's attention away from its poetic form. In the reworking, the more or less standard alexandrine yields to the much less frequently used long eight-foot line, which has a tendency, because of its length, to weaken the force and the reader's awareness of the rhyme pattern. In this connection, lines four and five are of particular interest, where, as a result of the finality of the caesura at the end of the sentence in line four and the enjambement between lines four and five, the normal form and balance of the sonnet quartet is radically disturbed. Furthermore, while the three temptations are, practically speaking, presented in the two quartets and the first tercet respectively, this carefully planned use of the formal divisions within the sonnet is at least partly obscured, for the point of division between each of these segments is effectively erased by the premature beginning of the second quartet in the middle of line four and the first tercet in the middle of line eight, as well as by the enjambements between four and five, and eight and nine. The separation between the first and the second tercets is, on the other hand, clear, but by now all ambiguities have already been resolved and there can no longer be any doubt that we are dealing with a poetic interpretation of the biblical word and not the word itself.

Not until the sestet, or at the very least the last line of the octet, is the true identity of the speaker of the sonnet revealed. But what of the temptations themselves, seen now in the light of this change in the reader's perspective? Perhaps so long as the "ich" of the sonnet is taken to be Jesus, it appears that a statement of the temptations, essentially intact despite some rephrasing, and Jesus' replies to them are actually given here. So, for example, in the first quartet the desert into which Jesus was led is mentioned, as are the sustenance of God's word and the contrast between the stones and the bread. Present in the second four lines are the three essential elements of the second temptation according to Matthew —the fall from the heights, the support of the angels, and the statement that God is not to be tempted. But when the sestet is reached and the façade falls away, these must be reconsidered in a new context. In what seems typical Gryphian fashion, we are forced to return to what we have already read and accepted, and to discover its meaning anew. Stated differently, the language of the poem must be considered on a two-fold level, that of the biblical word and that of the poetic word, in which latter case the poet adds a new dimension by means of a process of abstraction. On the one hand, the referent of Gryphius' "wüsten" of line one is the same as that of the biblical "Wüsten"; on the other hand, however, on the level of the poetic word, the concrete "Wüsten" of Matthew has been abstracted and exists here as a metaphor.

Gryphius' "raue wüsten" can be taken only as a metaphor for life itself, the "harte steine" as the problems with which man is beset during that life. Now that the identity of the speaker in the sonnet has been established, minor inconsistencies between the sonnet and the biblical text, changes as well as additions and omissions which might otherwise have passed without comment, take on a new significance. Satan has been depersonalized and does not appear by name in the octave as the tempter. Jesus' "Heb dich weg von mir Satan" (4: 10) is rendered "Weg! weg! hinweg du stoltzer geist!" by Gryphius. More important here for Gryphius, it would seem, is the fact that man's life in this world is to be considered as God's test of him. The temptation itself has undergone further changes. In the Scriptures, Jesus is actively challenged by Satan and chooses, because of his faith, not to accept the challenge. Faced with a specific physical need, the Son of God avoids making use of his miraculous powers to alleviate his physical suffering, pointing out that even in this life the spiritual is of greater importance than the physical. In the sonnet there is no challenge, and mortal man, with no miraculous powers at his disposal, stands necessarily by the very fact of his existence enmeshed in a world which is by nature a desert and seems to offer nothing good. While Jesus never hesitates for a moment in his emphasis on the importance of the spiritual over the merely physical, the spiritual values of the speaker in the poem have been at least temporarily shaken by the "harte steine" of his existence—it is a "matte seele" that looks to the word of God for sustenance and consolation.[3]

Nor is any challenge expressed in the second temptation of the sonnet, where in the Bible the devil attempts to goad Jesus into jumping from the pinnacle of the temple. Rather, in place of the

3. It seems likely that the imagery and ideas of lines three and four also have their source in the Bible. Cf. Psalms 80: 6, "Du [Gott] speisest sie mit Tranenbrod, und tränkest sie mit grossem Mass voll Tränen." The meaning of the sonnet lines would then seem to be that while God is the source of that which hinders and plagues man, he also creates that which helps (*alles Brot*). Cf. also Judges 16: 16, "Da sie ihn aber trieb mit ihren Worten alle Tage, und zerplagte ihn; ward seine Seele matt, bis an den Tod."

challenge is the reported will of the "devil," not to force him to test his powers or to tempt his God, but to plunge him "in den abgrund" of Hell. The biblical Satan urges Christ to see whether his God actually will send his angels to save the physical part of him from destruction. Gryphius, making use of the same imagery, is speaking of something else, the salvation of his soul.

In the sestet, which parallels the third biblical temptation, the images of Matthew have not become metaphor completely, but remain, at least in part, in their original concrete meanings. Here too, however, the poet adds an element not present in the Scriptures and stresses thereby the ever-present problem of *vanitas* and transience. But, although the wealth and splendor of the world remain concrete in the sonnet, the situation is no longer so specific. Gryphius' concern is rather with the danger of placing trust in that which is merely temporal and will ultimately vanish. The introduction in the first tercet of the theme of transience and the deception of the illusory "herrlichkeit der welt," the "prächtig auffgeschmücktes nichts" of which it consists—i.e., the problem of *Sein/Schein*—has already been prefigured by "listen" of line four. It is interesting that Gryphius was uncertain about this latter word. Although "listen" appears in the original edition of his works in 1639, Gryphius revised it to "lüsten" for the 1650 edition, which appeared in Strassburg. The 1657 edition retains "lüsten," but in the *Ausgabe letzter Hand* of 1663, "lüsten" is once again replaced by "listen," and so it appears both in the Welti and the Palm editions. We can only speculate about the reasons for such a change. As we have already suggested earlier in this study, the only valid method of approaching such matters entails recognition of the fact that often no single reason can be assumed for an author's revision, even if it be a question of only a single word. Furthermore, to attempt to arrive at one outstanding determining factor for a textual change without the express help of the author's comments is often futile. Nor can variants stemming from a poet's own hand be left a matter of whim. In this case, there seems to be no question of rhetoric involved in the change, no possible claim of a bowing to convention, to the impersonal rules of "poetry making" of the author's time, of an increasing objectivity in Gryphius and an almost necessarily resulting decrease in personal warmth and feeling. The poet thus cannot be charged with all the alleged esthetic crimes so often leveled against him even today where matters of the revisions of his lyric poetry are concerned. Yet there is a revision, and one which involves change of meaning.

Carl Hitzeroth, in his study of the religious lyric of Johann Heermann, points out among the characteristics of Silesian dialect that still remain in Heermann's poetry (even after that poet had attempted to cleanse his work of such traces in an apparent yielding to Opitz' admonitions against dialect forms) the frequent *i/ü* rhyme that Heermann so readily makes use of.[4] It is of course possible that Gryphius, in his change from "listen" to "lüsten," was moved by a similar compunction to conform to this policy. Manheimer indicates that there was apparently some inclination on Gryphius' part to accept some of Opitz' "rules," albeit the record of his actions in the revision of his poetry is far from consistent where such matters are concerned. In view of these facts, it also seems likely that, despite the problem of the rhyme, Gryphius felt even more strongly that the use of "lüsten" and the implication of sin brought about by partaking in physical pleasures would constitute too great a deviation from the biblical text at a time when the ambiguity concerning the identity of the speaker is still maintained, since the second temptation is not at all concerned with such matters. While "lüsten" would, to be sure, foreshadow the one side of the images of transience that occur in the sestet, with "listen" the poet actually comes closer to the heart of the matter, the element of deception in worldly pleasures and desires, an idea common to Gryphius and many of his contemporaries. It is a theme which then leads naturally and directly to the basic problem of *Sein/Schein*, illusion vs. reality, i.e., in Gryphius' frame of reference, the physical versus the spiritual, the temporal versus the eternal. Gryphius was by no means a mystic, yet he was certainly familiar with the tradition and literature of the medieval mystics; it is surely more than mere coincidence that "Wüste," in the mystical writings and later in the language of Pietism, is a term for *Gottesferne.*[5] And would not then the "steine" of line two, the problems facing man during his lifetime, represent the very material pleasures spoken of later in the first tercet? While the three temptations of Satan in Matthew remain essentially unrelated, although all aim at the same goal of shaking Jesus' faith, the three temptations of the sonnet bear in

4. *Johann Heermann* (Marburg, 1907), p. 108.
5. Cf. August Langen, *Der Wortschatz des deutschen Pietismus* (Tübingen, 1954), pp. 130, 171 ff.

common a single thematic thread. One wonders further whether the theme of deception and illusion itself is not intentionally mirrored in the uncertainty surrounding the identity of the speaker, which has already been discussed above.

The second tercet reverses the situation of the Bible completely—not Satan, but man challenges, boldly and with a strong faith in the efficacy of Divine aid. In line thirteen, with a paraphrase of the statements of Genesis 3: 15 and 1 John 3: 8, the Old Testament prophecy by Jahweh in Eden of the battle between man and the serpent of evil on earth, and the New Testament proclamation of the victory over evil through Jesus, Gryphius concludes with heavy emphasis on the conflict between sin and redemption. The sonnet begins with the problems of earthly existence, in which man is consoled by his faith, and ends with the anticipation of salvation, the ultimate result of this faith for the Lutheran Gryphius. In Matthew, Satan tempts the Son of God in a test of his own faith in his Messiahship. In Gryphius' sonnet, man's faith in the word of God is more closely connected with the question of sin and salvation. What is presented in the Bible as a series of historical, concrete events is abstracted by the poet. The setting is changed from the confrontation of Jesus in the desert with the devil to that of man in a world of sin where salvation is attained by passive resistance to the evil about him and by faith in divine help. Once again, the poet, by using a biblical passage as a thematic point of departure, creates from the biblical references his own context and frame of reference on a different level of meaning; of the biblical text is born by means of the poetic word a statement of his own personal faith.

# 8

## Auff den Sontag
## deß wachsenden Wortes

Although most of the one hundred *Sonn-und Feiertagssonette* of Andreas Gryphius do not rank among the best of his lyrics, a study of them is nonetheless fruitful for any examination of the poet's style, for in these poems we can catch a glimpse of the significance for Gryphius of the Scriptures as a source for his poetry as well as some insight into the very process of fashioning a work of art. In addition, by a comparison of these Gryphius sonnets with *geistliche Lieder* of other seventeenth-century poets similarly based upon biblical texts in accordance with the church calendar, we can gain some knowledge of Gryphius' position historically within this tradition. Perhaps most important, we may learn whether there is, in an age often cited for its submission to norms, in a literary period supposedly noted for its subordination to tradition rather than for its emphasis on individualism, some trait in Gryphius' poetry which sets him off from his contemporaries. Important, then, is not so much the fact *that*, but rather the question *how*, he works within that tradition, what he takes from and lends to it. Our interest lies in the manner in which he makes use of a conventional mode, making it serve his own ends, and, specifically here, in exactly what function the biblical texts serve in the creation of his poetry. Considered below as examples of that tradition are one of the *Episteln der Sonntage und fürnembsten Feste des gantzen Jahrs* by Martin Opitz, written in 1623, and one of Johann Heermann's *Sontags und Fest-Evangelia* of 1636. I have chosen a poem by Opitz because of this poet's obvious influence on German literature of the seventeenth century and a selection from Heermann's works because of the similarities often claimed, by critics of Gryphius as well as by students of Heermann's poetry, between the religious lyrics of the two authors. The following text by Opitz is based on Isaiah 60. The sections of the Bible concerned are printed directly thereafter:

### An der Heiligen Drey König Tage
#### (On the Day of the Three Wise Men)

Brich auff und werde Liechte,
Laß gehn die Nacht zu nichte,
Dein Liecht kömpt her zu dir;
Die Herrligkeit deß Herren
Gläntzt prächtig weit und ferren
Und zeigt sich über dir.

Zwar finster ist die Erde,
Der armen Heyden Herde
Ligt tunckel weit und breit;
Dich hat der Herr, dein Leben,
Dein Heil und Trost, umgeben
Mit grosser Herrligkeit.

Heb auff, heb dein Gesichte,
Das Volck folgt deinem Liechte,
Die Welt kömpt gantz zu dir;
Sie hat von dir vernommen,
Die Söhn und Tochter kommen
Und suchen deine Zier.

Dein Hertze wird dir wallen,
Wenn die kömpt zu Gefallen
Die Anzahl umb das Meer;
Du wirst die Augen weiden
Am Volcke deiner Heyden,
So gantz dringt zu dir her.

Die Völcker auff der Erden,
So je beschienen werden
Durchs klare Sonnenliecht,
Die Sollen dein Liecht kennen,
Zum Glantze frölich rennen,
Der auß der Höhe bricht.

Es kommen alle Seelen
Aus Epha mit Camelen,
Mit Läuffern Midian;
Gold wird dir Saba bringen
Und Weyrauch; es wird singen
Dein Lob ein jederman.

(Arise and become light,
Let disappear the night,
Your light descends to you;
The splendor of our Lord
Shines brightly wide and far
And now appears above you.

Dark is o'er the earth,
The crowd of hapless heathen
Lies darkly all about;
The Lord surrounds you, your life,
Your solace and salvation
With the splendor of His majesty.

Lift up, lift up your face,
The people heed your light,
The whole world comes to you;
It has had word of you,
Your sons and daughters come
To view your rich adornment.

Your heart will overflow
When at your wish appears
The crowd about the sea;
And you shall feast your eyes
On multitudes of heathen,
Who make their way to you.

All peoples of the earth
Whoe'er were shone upon

By shining rays of sun,
Shall recognize your light,
Run joyful toward its radiance
That gleams down from the heights.

All the souls shall come,
From Epha with their camels,
The runners out of Midia;
From Sheba gold they'll bring
And frankincense; and all
Will sing your praise in joy.)[1]

## Isaiah 60

1. Mache dich auff, werde liechte, Denn dein Liecht kompt, und die Herrligkeit des HERRN gehet auff über dir.
2. Denn sihe, finsternis bedeckt das Erdreich, und tunckel die Völcker, Aber vber dir gehet auff der HERR und seine Herrligkeit erscheinet vber dir.
3. VND die Heiden werden in deinem Liecht wandeln, vnd die Könige im Glantz der vber dir auffgehet.
4. Hebe deine augen auff vnd sihe vmbher, diese alle versamlet, komen zu dir, Deine Söne werden von ferne komen, vnd deine Töchter zur seiten erzogen werden.
5. Denn wirstu deine lust sehen vnd ausbrechen, und dein Hertz wird sich wundern vnd ausbreiten, wenn sich die menge am Meer zu dir bekeret, vnd die macht der Heiden zu dir kompt.
6. Denn die menge der Kamelen wird dich bedecken, die Leuffer aus Midian und Epha, Sie werden aus Saba alle komen, gold vnd weyrauch bringen, vnd des HERRN lob verkündigen.

Basically, Opitz' song is simply a paraphrase of the first six verses of the biblical chapter, a retelling of the story, at times with rather extensive elaboration as in the third stanza, which corresponds roughly to sections of verses three and four. At other places, however, whole phrases and lines are taken intact from the Scriptures, and the six individual stanzas of the song correspond exactly to the six biblical verses. Most striking is the fact that the individual words, phrases, and images taken from the biblical text are re-

1. Martin Opitz, *Weltliche und geistliche Dichtung,* ed. D. Desterley, in *Deutsche Nationalliteratur,* vol. 27 (Berlin and Stuttgart, n.d.), p. 208.

peated here always in exactly the same situations, so that the poem never does go beyond that text by the addition of ideas or images not already present in it. The farthest that Opitz goes is to emphasize and extend certain basic images or themes, like "Liecht" in stanza three and in stanza one. Here he contrasts this image with "Nacht" somewhat before the Bible, in fact, introduces the idea of darkness. But all of this remains on the level of simple elaboration, the task—and it can hardly be viewed as very much more than an exercise—of putting into rhyming meter as many as possible of the elements offered in these six verses of the Bible and remaining as close as possible to the original  text. There is no attempt to create anew. The biblical text itself is the *raison d'être* of the song, its meaning is the meaning of the Scriptures, and the poet stands above his work, objectively refashioning and slightly revising, but without himself interpreting or becoming actively involved.

The *Kirchenlied* selected from Johann Heermann's works is based upon Matthew 13. Both the song and the text from Matthew follow:

Am sechsten Sonntage nach dem Fest der H. drei Könige
(On the Sixth Sunday after the Festival of the Three Wise Men)

1. Wem soll ich gleich
Das Himmelreich
Allhier auf Erden schätzen?
Ein Senfkorn kann
Das zeigen an,
Das wir in Acker setzen.

2. Wird doch so klein
Kein Körnlein sein
Fast unter allem Samen,
Wenn ich sie dir
Gleich rechne für
Und nenne gar mit Namen.

3. Doch wenns zunimmt
Und Kraft bekömmt
Da pflegt sichs auszubreiten
Und wird ein Baum,
Der grossen Raum
Begehrt zu allen Seiten.

4. Wird sein gewahr
Der Vogel Schar
Und sieht die Aest aufsteigen,
So fleugt sie zu
Und suchet Ruh
Da unter seinen Zweigen.

5. Nichts ist so sehr
Als Christi Lehr
In dieser Welt verachtet.
Sein Glanz und Schein
Ist schlecht und klein,
Dem stets der Feind nachtrachtet.

6. Doch muß sie oft
Auch unverhofft
Durch vieler Herzen dringen
Und weit und breit
Der Christenheit
Viel tausend Früchte bringen.

7. Hält mans gleich schlecht
Machts doch gerecht
Die, so daran fest glauben.
Gesetz und Werk
Hat keine Stärk
Aus dir den Tod zu treiben.

8. Wol dem, der sich
Beständiglich
Bei Christi Wort läßt finden.
Er hat da Schutz
Und kann den Trutz
Des Teufels überwinden.

9. Hilf, Jesu Christ,
Zu jeder Frist,
Daß dein Wort bei uns grüne.
Gib allzeit Kraft
Und solchen Saft,
Der ihm zu Wachsen diene.

10. Wer sich ausrüst
Mit Macht und List

Und will sein Wachsen wehren,
Den wollst du bald,
Herr, mit Gewalt
In deinem Zorn verzehren.

(To what on earth
Can be compared
The Heavenly Kingdom with its worth?
That kingdom's like
The mustard seed
Which we sow in the fields.

If I should try
To name them all
Then you would clearly see
That none among
All the seeds
Is quite so small as this one.

But when it grows
And its strength increases
It then begins to spread
And becomes a tree,
Whose branches then
Extend in all directions.

Should flocks of birds
Now glimpse its form
And see its branches rise,
They fly thereto
And seek out peace
Among its leafy branches.

In this world nothing's
More despised
Than Christ's own words and teachings.
His radiant light
Is dim and faint
For one pursued by foes.

But it does often
Unexpected
Pierce the hearts of many,
And far and wide

For Christendom
Bear many thousand fruits.

Though oft reproved
They are yet wise
Who trust in this completely.
Law and works
Have not the power
To rescue you from death.

Blessed is he
Who constantly
Holds fast to Jesus' words.
He is protected,
And will o'ercome
The Devil's spite and challenge.

Help, Jesus Christ,
At every time
Let your word flourish in us.
Give of your strength
And nourishment,
So needed for its growth.

Who girds himself
With might and guile
And will prevent its growth,
Him you will soon,
O Lord, by force
Consume in vengeful wrath.)[2]

## Matthew 13

1. AN dem selbigen tage gieng Jhesus aus dem hause, vnd satzte sich an das Meer.
2. Vnd es versamlet sich viel Volcks zu jm, also, das er in das Schiff trat, vnd sas, vnd alles Volck stund am vfer.
3. Vnd er redet zu jnen mancherley, durch Gleichnisse, vnd sprach, Sihe, es gieng ein Seeman aus zu seen.
4. Vnd in dem er seet, fiel etlichs an den Weg, Da kamen die Vogel vnd frassens auff.
5. Etlichs fiel in das Steinichte, da es nicht viel erden hatte,

2. *Geistliche Lieder der evangelischen Kirche aus dem 17. und der 1. Hälfte des 18. Jahrhunderts von Dichtern aus Schlesien und den umliegenden Landschaften verfaßt*, ed. Julius Mützell, vol. 1 (Braunschweig, 1858), p. 105.

vnd gieng bald auff, darumb, das es nicht tieffe erden hatte.

6. Als aber die Sonne auffgieng verwelcket es vnd dieweil es nicht Wurtzel hatte, ward es dürre.

7. Etlichs fiel vnter die Dörnen, Vnd die Dörnen wuchsen auff, vnd ersticktens.

8. Etlichs fiel auff ein gut Land, vnd trug Frucht, Etlichs hundertfeltig, etlichs sechzigfeltig, etlichs dreissigfeltig.

9. Wer ohren hat zu hören, der höre.

10. VND die Jünger tratten zu jm, vnd sprachen, Warumb redest du zu jnen durch Gleichnisse?

11. Er antwortet, vnd sprach, Euch ists gegeben, das jr das geheimnis des Himelreichs vernemet, Diesen aber ists nicht gegeben.

12. Denn wer da hat, dem wird gegeben, das er die fülle habe, Wer aber nicht hat, von dem wird auch genomen, das er hat.

13. Darumb rede ich zu jnen durch Gleichnisse, Denn mit sehenden Augen, sehen sie nicht, vnd mit hörenden Ohren, hören sie nicht, denn sie verstehen es nicht.

14. Vnd vber jnen wird die weissagung Jsaie erfüllet, die da sagt, Mit den Ohren werdet jr hören, vnd werdet es nicht verstehen, vnd mit sehenden Augen werdet jr sehen, vnd werdet es nicht vernemen.

15. Denn dieses Volcks Hertz ist verstockt, vnd jre Ohren hören vbel, vnd jre Augen schlummern, Auff das sie nicht der mal eins mit den Augen sehen, vnd mit den Ohren hören, vnd mit dem Hertzen verstehen, vnd sich bekeren, das ich jnen hülffe.

16. ABer selig sind ewer Augen, das sie sehen, vnd ewr Ohren, das sie hören.

17. Warlich ich sage euch, Viel Propheten vnd Gerechten haben begert, zu sehen, das jr sehet, vnd habens nicht gesehen, Vnd zu hören, das jr höret, vnd habens nicht gehöret.

18. SO höret nun ir diese Gleichnis von dem Seeman.

19. Wenn jemand das wort von dem Reich höret, vnd nicht verstehet, So kompt der Arge, vnd reisset es hin, was da geseet ist in sein hertz, vnd der ists, der an dem Wege geseet ist.

20. Der aber auff das Steinichte geseet ist, der ists, wenn jemand das Wort höret, vnd dasselbige bald auffnimpt mit freuden.

21. Aber er hat nicht wurtzeln in jm, sondern ist wetter-

wendisch, Wenn sich trübsal vnd verfolgung erhebt vmb des
Worts willen, So ergert er sich balde.

22. Der aber vnter die Dörnen geseet ist, der ists, Wenn
jemand das Wort höret, Vnd die sorge dieser Welt, vnd
betrug des Reichtums, ersticket das Wort, vnd bringet nicht
Frucht.

23. Der aber in das gute Land geseet ist, der ists, Wenn
jemand das Wort höret, vnd verstehet es, vnd denn auch
Frucht bringet, Vnd etlicher tregt hundertfeltig, etlicher
aber sechzigfeltig, etlicher dreissigfeltig.

24. ER legt jnen ein ander Gleichnis fur, vnd sprach. Das
Himelreich ist gleich einem Menschen, der guten Samen
auff seinen Acker seet.

25. Da aber die Leute schlieffen, kam sein Feind, vnd seete
Vnkraut zwischen den Weitzen, vnd gieng dauon.

26. Da nu das Kraut wuchs, vnd Frucht bracht, Da fand sich
auch das Vnkraut.

27. Da tratten die Knechte zu dem Hausvater, vnd sprachen,
Herr, hastu nicht guten Samen auff deinen acker geseet?
Wo her hat er denn das Vnkraut?

28. Er sprach zu jnen, Das hat der Feind gethan. Da sprachen
die Knechte, Wiltu denn, das wir hin gehen vnd es
ausgetten?

29. Er sprach, Nein, Auff das jr nicht zu gleich den Weitzen
mit ausreuffet, so jr das Vnkraut ausgettet.

30. Lasset beides mit einander wachsen, bis zu der Erndte,
Vnd umb der erndte zeit, wil ich zu den Schnittern sagen,
Samlet zuuor das Vnkraut, vnd bindet es in Bündlin, das
man es verbrenne, Aber den Weitzen samlet mir in meine
Schewren.

31. EIn ander Gleichnis leget er jnen fur, vnd sprach. Das
Himelreich ist gleich einem Senffkorn, das ein  Mensch nam,
vnd seet auff seinen Acker,

32. Welches das kleinest ist vnter allem Samen, Wenn es aber
erwechst, so ist es das grössest vnter dem Kol, vnd wird ein
Bawm, das die Vögel vnter dem himel komen vnd wonen
vnter seinen zweigen.

33. EIn ander Gleichnis redet er zu jnen. Das Himelreich ist
einem Sawerteig gleich, den ein Weib nam, vnd vermenget
jn vnter drey scheffel Melhs, bis das es ger durchsewrt ward.

34. SOlchs alles redet Jhesus durch Gleichnis zu dem Volck,
vnd on gleichnisse redet er nicht zu jnen.

35. Auff das erfüllet würde, das gesagt ist durch den

Propheten, der da spricht, Ich wil meinen mund auffthun in Gleichnissen, vnd wil aussprechen die Heimligkeit von anfang der Welt.

36. DA lies Jhesus das Volck von sich, vnd kam heim. Vnd seine Jungere tratten zu jm, vnd sprachen, Deute uns die Gleichnisse vom unkraut auff dem Acker.

37. Er anwort, vnd sprach zu jnen, Des menschen Son ists, der da guten Samen seet.

38. Der Acker ist die Welt. Der gute Same, sind die kinder des Reichs. Das Vnkraut, sind die kinder der bosheit.

39. Der Feind der sie seet, ist der Teufel. Die Erndte, ist das ende der Welt. Die Schnitter, sind die Engel.

40. Gleich wie man nu das Vnkraut ausgettet vnd mit fewr verbrennet, So wirds auch am ende dieser Welt gehen.

41. Des menschen Son wird seine Engel senden, vnd sie werden samlen aus seinem Reich alle Ergernisse, vnd die da vnrecht tun,

42. vnd werden sie in den Fewr ofen werffen, Da wird sein heulen vnd zeenklappen.

43. Denn werden die Gerechten leuchten, wie die Sonne in jres Vaters reich. Wer ohren hat zu hören, der höre.

44. ABErmal ist gleich das Himelreich einem verborgen Schatz im acker, welchen ein Mensch fand, vnd verbarg jn, Vnd gieng hin fur freuden vber dem selbigen, vnd verkaufft alles was er hatte, vnd kauffte den Acker.

45. ABermal ist gleich das Himelreich einem Kauffman, der gute Perlen suchte,

46. Vnd da er eine köstliche Perlen fand, gieng er hin, vnd verkauffte alles was er hatte, vnd kauffte die selbigen.

47. ABermal ist gleich das Himelreich einem netze, das ins Meer geworffen ist, da mit man allerley Gattung fehet.

48. Wenn es aber vol ist, so ziehen sie es eraus an das vfer, sitzen vnd lesen die guten in ein Gefess zusamen, Aber die faulen werffen sie weg.

49. Also wird es auch am ende der Welt gehen, Die Engel werden ausgehen, vnd die Bösen von den Gerechten scheiden,

50. vnd werden sie in den Fewr ofen werffen, Da wird heulen vnd zeenklappen sein.

51. VNd Jhesus sprach zu jnen, Habt jr das alles verstanden? Sie sprachen, Ja HErr.

52. Da sprach er, Darumb ein jglicher Schrifftgelerter zum Himelreich gelert, ist gleich einem Hausuatter, der aus seinem schat, Newes vnd Altes erfur tregt.

53. VND es begab sich, da Jhesus diese Gleichnisse volendet hatte, Gieng er von dannen,
54. vnd kam in sein Vaterland, vnd leret sie in jren Schulen, also auch, das sie sich entsatzten, vnd sprachen, Wo her kompt diesem solche Weisheit vnd Thatten?
55. Ist er nicht eines Zimmermans son? Heisst nicht seine mutter Maria? Vnd seine Brüdere, Jakob vnd Josef, vnd Simon, vnd Judas,
56. vnd seine Schwestern sind sie nicht alle bey uns? Wo her kompt jm denn das alles?
57. vnd ergerten sich an jm. Jhesus aber sprach zu jnen, Ein Prophet gilt nirgend weniger, denn in seinem Vaterland vnd in seinem Hause.
58. Vnd er that daselbs nicht viel Zeichen, Vmb ires vnglaubens willen.

The aspects of the *Kirchenlied* observed in Opitz, the strict reiteration of the biblical passage, both in its content and its viewpoint, the severe conformity throughout all ten stanzas to one rhythm and meter, the great pains apparently taken with the rather mechanical rhyming, the author's fitting of the words of the Bible to the lips of a congregation, are just as clearly the dominant factors in Heermann. The biblical comparison of the mustard seed and the kingdom of heaven is expanded to fill out the first four stanzas, while the remaining six are devoted to an emphatic reminder of the necessity, for salvation, of the acceptance of Jesus' teaching. The tone of the whole remains prophetic and admonishing, and the emphasis, in the final stanza, lies with God's punishment of those who actively resist His precepts and fail to act in accordance with them.

Let us now turn to Gryphius' sonnet on the same passage:

Kein Körnlein ist so klein / als Senff vor uns zu schätzen /
  Doch / wenn es in die Schoß der feuchten Erden fällt
  So wurtzelts eilend eyn / und keimet in die Welt,
Und wird ein hoher Baum / der rund umb allen Plätzen
Deß Schattens Lust außtheilt. Denn eylet sich zu setzen
  Manch Vogel umb den Ast / der sich da sicher hält
  Alsbald der Himmel plitzt, alsbald man nach ihm stellt.
Ihn kan kein Wind / kein Sturm / kein Jägergarn verletzen.
  So scheint deß Höchsten Wort in Menschen Augen klein;
  Doch kom'ts einmal ins Hertz, so nim'ts die Sinnen eyn

Und läßt bald Stock und Zweig und Blütt' und Früchte
           [schauen.
Der unter diesem Baum bey trüber Wetters-Zeit
Ihm Zuflucht außerkiest / dem wird vors Windes Streit /
Vors Teuffels Vogel-Netz / vor's Todes Pfeyl nicht grauen.
          (*Werke* 1: 195–96)


(There is no seed on earth as small as the mustard seed,
But when it makes its bed in the soft earth's moist bosom,
It quickly then takes root and sprouts into the world,
Becomes a towering tree which round about the ground
Its pleasing shade extends. Among its leafy branches
Then rush the birds to sit, who take their refuge there
When lightning flashes down or hunters seek their prey.
No wind nor storm nor hunter's snare can do it injury.
Likewise the word of God may seem in man's eyes small;
But if it pierce the heart, it soon dominates the mind,
And brings to blossom now twig, now branch and flower and
          [fruit.
Whoever refuge seeks in time of raging storms
Amidst this tree's full boughs need fear no whistling wind,
Nor Devil's cunning snares, nor even Death's sharp arrows.)


The poem is based on one parable of Matthew 13, that of the mustard seed in verses 31 and 32. At first glance the sonnet does indeed seem to be a close retelling of these verses, containing all the essential elements of the biblical passage and nothing more. A closer examination, however, discloses that the content, the meaning, and the tone of the Matthew text have undergone a change, a fact that may not be immediately apparent because of the careful structuring of the sonnet. The sonnet form is well suited to the treatment of the parable, and Gryphius is careful to make the most of this fact, both for emphasis and for the achievement of an exact balance within the poem between the elements of comparison. Thus the octet is completely devoted to a description of the growth of the mustard seed, the sestet to the second member of the comparison. In the parable itself, the similarity between the mustard seed and the kingdom of heaven is first simply stipulated, then supported by a description of the *Senfkorn* and its growth from the smallest of seeds to a tree of extraordinary size. In the sonnet each element in the description of the growth of the mustard seed in the octave finds its exact counterpart in the precise explanation of the sestet.

Upon casual reading, the sonnet, then, does not appear to deviate from its thematic source. Within the first four and one-half lines of the poem, although there are allusions to other verses of Matthew, no image, save one (indeed, hardly a word), occurs which does not appear somewhere in the chapter, and this one image, when it is inserted in line five, is not immediately conspicuous. Once again in this sonnet Gryphius' method reveals his effective use of and reliance on the development of patterns. Such patterns, once established, create in the reader a sense of anticipation fostered by expectations which are in turn born, consciously or unconsciously, of his own mental associations. The poet is then able to control his emphasis by causing certain elements to recur regularly, by maintaining a pattern which has been carefully prepared, or by deviating from that pattern. Here such a pattern has been created within the first four lines of the octave, that of a close conformity to the biblical source, so that the reader who is familiar with the biblical chapter is lulled, as it were, into expecting no radical divergence from the Scriptures in the lines that follow. And indeed, when a new element, at first in the form of a new image, does appear, it does not seem to be a radically new addition. On the contrary, it blends so well and so logically with the old that one is not at first fully aware of it as something new. In lines two and three there is a clear reference to another parable from Matthew in the phrases "wenn es in die Schoß der feuchten erden fällt" and "so wurtzelts eilend ein und keimet in die welt," which Gryphius' reader, *bibelfest* as he is, will also recognize easily. More important, however, though it very likely goes unnoticed until at least the following three lines are read, is the image of shade in line five: "der rund umb allen Plätzen / Deß Schattens Lust außtheilt." While until this point in the poem Gryphius had borrowed ideas, images, and individual words and phrases from other verses than 31 and 32, "Schatten(s)" is one, introduced here unobtrusively, which does not occur at all in any of the verses of this chapter. It could, of course, be dismissed as simply a logical extension of the central image of the tree, as embellishment or elaboration without further significance. But Gryphius is a careful poet, as the many revisions undertaken in virtually all of his poems testify, and this image of shade, which existed already in the earlier version, "Theilt kühle schatten aus," is one which, for whatever reason, he clearly wished to retain. If for a moment we consider the parable of the mustard seed itself and compare it with the first eight lines of the sonnet, it becomes clear that this simple insertion of one more characteristic of the tree contains in fact the germ of a concept which is foreign to the biblical passage but constitutes the central meaning of the poem.

Certainly it would not do to offer here a dogmatic interpretation of the parable. Nevertheless, some explanation and consideration of the various interpretations are necessary at this point. It should be noted first that the subject of all the parables found in Matthew 13 is either "the kingdom of heaven" (*das Himmelreich*) or "the word of the kingdom" (*das Wort vom Reich*). Commentators have explained the meaning of the term "kingdom of heaven" in a variety of ways since the Reformation, but it would seem clear from the context of this chapter, from the parables in it taken as a whole, that the meaning here is prophetic, that it signifies that kingdom which is to be attained only in a life after death.[3] The kingdom has been construed also as the true reign of God on earth, the onset of which coincides with the appearance of Jesus, and as a symbol for the church itself in its earthly form.[4] For Matthew, however, neither of the latter two explanations holds. The parable of the mustard seed makes a comparison between the kingdom of heaven and the tiny seed, the one point common to both being the enormous and unexpected growth from the smallest, most insignificant beginnings. Some commentators have maintained that the emphasis, and the real point of comparison, lies rather in the concept of the inevitability of growth and have referred to the parable of the leaven and the bread in verse thirty-three as supporting evidence. In the mustard seed parable, however, the surprising size is so clearly stressed that it would be difficult to consider anything else as the real core of the verses.

If now the parable and Gryphius' sonnet are considered together first with respect to their treatment of the size of the full-grown tree, an interesting shift of emphasis is noted. In the Scrip-

3. Cf. verses 47–49, where the kingdom is likened to a net cast into the sea, which, when full, is withdrawn so that the good fish can be separated from the bad, the latter to be cast away again. There follows in 49, "Also wird auch am ende der Welt gehen, / Die Engel werden ausgehen, vnd die Bösen von den Gerechten scheiden. . . ." Cf. also verses 24–30, 37–43.

4. For information on the various interpretations, I have used John Bright's *The Kingdom of God* (Nashville, 1952), especially chapter 8.

tures, the seed becomes a tree reckoned as "the largest among the herbs" ("das grössest vnter dem Kol"), so large, in fact, that all the birds of the heavens can sit among its branches ("das die Vögel vnter dem himel komen vnd wonen vnter seinen zweigen"). A representation of the birds sitting under the tree forms a part of the sonnet also, but the stress is no longer on the size of the tree and the large number of birds that it can, as a result, accommodate: "Denn eylet sich zu setzen / Manch Vogel umb den Ast."

In describing the size of the tree itself, Gryphius says merely that it becomes "ein hoher Baum." The only other characteristic of the tree given is that of the shade cast. The reason for the introduction of the shade becomes clear as the following lines are read, for the idea of the safety and protection afforded the birds—here from the rays of the sun—is elaborated at length in the remaining three and one-half lines of the octet. Here the protection offered by the tree is of central importance, a promise which is strengthened by the repetition of the storm images throughout two lines, and once again reinforced by the strong, clipped stresses of line eight. The element introducing this theme of protection and safety, although it may not at first seem to be a new image when taken in the context of the preceding lines, is itself stressed in line five by the combination of its first position and the enjambement of lines four to five—the first of the sonnet. Adding to this emphasis is the complete stop directly after it at the third-foot caesura, the only such complete stop in the middle of a line in the entire sonnet. In line eight there is a break in the rhythm pattern. In the previous seven lines Gryphius has used a fairly regular alexandrine. Here, instead of a single caesura after the third foot, as is found in every other line of the poem with the possible exception of line two, there is a double caesura after the second and third feet. The forceful rhythm of the line is heightened by the threefold repetition of "kein," a word which, according to the metrical pattern of the alexandrine, should take an accent in none of its three occurrences. At the same time, the object pronoun "Ihn," in the first position, receives at least a secondary stress. The verb "kan" meanwhile carries its own stress by virtue of its being the second syllable of an iambic foot. The facts that, before the line was revised, "Ihn" did not stand first and that, as a result, the first foot read more like a normal iamb indicate once again Gryphius' care in matters of rhythm. The line is further noteworthy because of the uninterrupted sequence of seven one-syllable words; for the first eight syllables of the thirteen-syllable line there are no unaccented final syllables that would be naturally unstressed. The result of all this is a strongly emphatic line whose inflection continues to rise past the third-foot caesura until the end of the fourth foot. Indeed, the two caesuras, far from impeding the forward movement of the rhythm and the rising inflection, contribute to both. Although they do cause a momentary pause, in their function here of connecting the elements of a series they anticipate its completion and also that of the thought unit. That Gryphius intended to stress this line in his revision becomes apparent when it is compared with the original line eight: "Doch mag ihn dar kein wind, kein jäger-garn verletzen." Nor can the fact be overlooked that this line, which is metrically and rhythmically set off from the preceding seven lines and which contains the most emphatic formulation of the idea of the tree as a place of refuge, is the eighth line of the sonnet. It is thus strongly accentuated again by its very position at the point of division between octet and sestet, all the more so in this sonnet since the separation between the two sections of the octet itself has been effectively bridged by the enjambement of lines four to five. Thus four full lines of the octave are given over, with ever-increasing intensity, to the idea of the tree as a haven from the dangers of man as well as of nature.

Not until the opening line of the sestet is it made clear to what the mustard seed and the tree into which it grows are to be compared, although once again the reader's knowledge of Matthew will lead him to expect that the kingdom of heaven is to be the second term. But here Gryphius makes a second change in his version of the parable, for the mustard seed is taken to represent the word of God, "deß Höchsten Wort." As the poem proceeds, it becomes clear that Gryphius has made use of the biblical passage to express his own needs and apparently his own personal confession of faith. Using the words of the Scriptures only to the extent that they fit the pattern of these needs and beliefs, he emerges with a guide for the concrete life of the individual, while the biblical passage concerns itself with the fate of man collectively in eternity. All that is prophetic in the biblical passage is omitted in the sonnet. The idea of man's punishment at the hand of the Divine if he refuses to accept the word of God, stressed so by Heermann, is not present at all. While the biblical parable is limited to a description of physical dimensions, in the sonnet sestet the tree becomes a metaphor, and all references to size must be taken figuratively. The essential point in the poem is the protective power of God's word. This power is not automatic, however, but depends for its effectiveness on a turning inward, an internalization of the Divine word. While the parable treats of external physical growth, Gryphius' concern is with an inner spiritual growth marked by a quasi-mystical union of God's word and the individual's inner being, a union in which the senses are absorbed by the all-suffusing Word.

For Gryphius, then, it appears that, although a knowledge of the biblical model is necessary for a complete understanding of the poem, the mere retelling of the Scriptures does not constitute an end in itself. The Bible serves him often as a tool, as the raw material of which a poem is to be forged, and particularly as a source of metaphor. While the themes of the original text appear in the sonnets also, the central theme of a poem may be quite different than the chapter on which it is based. Both the fact and the manner of this synthesis of the scriptural word and the poetic word, the personal element contributed by the poet which solidifies the bonding of the two, have too often gone unnoticed in the critical literature concerning the *Sonn-und Feiertagssonette*.

But if, in the sonnet just discussed, the meaning of the poem lies in the protection to be found in the word of God, what is this protective power to serve against? In the octet the birds are protected by a real tree from both the threat of the elements and that of the hunter. In the sestet the individual is protected by a metaphorical tree from metaphorical storms and a metaphorical arrow of death. The image of the storm has been popular in literature for centuries, and it appears countless times in Gryphius' works as a symbol for the tribulations of life. Man often assumes the role of a storm-tossed craft, buffeted by raging winds and towering waves upon the turbulent waters. Adamant as he is in his denunciation of worldly things as "eitell," the recurrent Gryphius problem seems to be to find a way of life free from the temptation to partake of the very pleasures of this life he so strongly attempts to negate completely. It would have been convenient, of course, if Hermann Palm's apparently spurious variant for line fourteen, the reading "teuffels pfeil" for "Todes Pfeyl," had proved valid; we might then have argued that the original 'Todes Pfeyl" had signified death, spiritual and/or physical, at the conclusion of physical life on earth, but that this allusion is removed in the revision, which would stress more the temptations faced in this life. Nevertheless, it seems clear from the phrasing of the sestet as it stands that the protection Gryphius hopes to find in "deß Höchsten Wort" is from the spiritually destructive, because seductive, human involvements in this world. It does not seem to be enough, that is, to know that the sinful descend to hell and the righteous ascend to heaven—or even to know what it is that makes one righteous. The problem is, rather, how to achieve and maintain that righteousness in this world. Elsewhere Gryphius comments on the need to race through life "mit schnellem Geist" so as to escape its bonds, to raise "den freyen Geist" above all, in order to somehow live in this world and yet above it. It would seem that it is freedom from these temptations and a way to this kind of existence that Gryphius seeks to find in the word of God.

Thus does the emphasis shift in the sonnet away from the prophetic elements of the gospel and toward the here and now, centering on life itself, for it is there, after all, that Gryphius faces his greatest dilemma.

# 9

# Gryphius as a Meditative Poet

In his recent essay Hans-Henrik Krummacher considers in detail several of Andreas Gryphius' long-neglected *Sonn-und Feiertags-sonette* for the first time in this century since Manheimer's diligent study of the lyric poems in 1904.[1] In the article Krummacher seeks to find a direct source for many of the themes and images of the sonnets in the prayers of Johann Arndt's *Paradiesgärtlein*. Such a view would substantiate Paul Böckmann's long-held contention that much of German Baroque literature, and Gryphius' poetry in particular, has deep roots in the tradition of the then immensely popular *Gebets- und Erbauungsliteratur*.[2] Aside from the difficulties involved in proving conclusively a specific reliance on Arndt, in some cases because of possible multiple common sources, Krummacher does seem to have established a connection strong enough to call for further study. He does not, however, concern himself with matters of technique and style, many elements of which certainly cannot be traced back to the *Paradiesgärtlein*. In this respect it would

1. "Andreas Gryphius und Johann Arndt. Zum Verständnis der 'Sonn-und Feiertags-Sonette,' " in *Formenwandel. Festschrift für Paul Böckmann* (Hamburg, 1964), pp. 116–37.
2. *Formgeschichte der deutschen Dichtung* (Hamburg, 1949), especially pp. 318–34.

be profitable to examine the possible role played by another, related tradition and to consider those features of Gryphius' poetry which lend support to a view of him as a meditative poet, or at least as a poet who makes use of certain methods and techniques that characterize the practice of meditation.

Although both Krummacher and Dietrich Walter Jöns[3] occasionally use the words *Meditation* and *meditieren* in their discussions of Gryphius' lyric, they obviously do not intend these terms in the very precise meaning that, for example, Louis Martz uses in his book *The Poetry of Meditation*.[4] Gryphius' poetry is a poetry of the mind, and throughout there is what can be called loosely a generally meditative or contemplative quality, the indication of a kind of inner searching. Very likely it is this tone that Krummacher and Jöns have perceived when they write of meditation. Here, however, we shall be concerned with something much more specific—the application to poetry of the methods of formal meditation, as it was practiced in sixteenth- and seventeenth-century Europe. Martz demonstrates convincingly how, guided by the *Spiritual Exercises* of Loyola and other works of the Jesuits and their counterparts in this tradition, the continental art of meditation coalesced with the literary tradition of the Rennaissance in England to become one of the fundamental organizing principles behind that body of poetry that has usually been called "metaphysical." Whether he will or not, Gryphius, of course, lives in close contact with the tradition of formal meditation, the origins of which extend well back into the Middle Ages. Before Loyola, such meditation was advocated by Calvin and Luther, and after the Reformation the practice was urged and carried out by Catholic and Protestant alike. Suitable manuals of prayer were available everywhere on the continent. Martz points out that, although the practice of meditation continued uninterrupted throughout the centuries, one of the periods in which it particularly flourished and was most widespread coincides exactly with the most fruitful years of English religious poetry in the seventeenth century, a time which coincidentally directly precedes and in part parallels Gryphius' most productive years. He has shown how, in theme, structure, and tone, much of that poetry bears a remarkable resemblance to specific sections of various meditational exercises, while occasionally

3. *Das "Sinnen-Bild,"* pp. 180–83.
4. New Haven, 1965.

an individual poem seems to reflect the entire sequence of a single meditation.

In the Jesuit writings of the sixteenth century, the methods of meditation are elaborately described, and the religious are urged to practice these methods as a part of their everyday life according to well-defined prescriptions. Although the meditative act is not in itself a part of a mystical experience, the possibilities for its application to the mystical process are obvious. Through this willed act of contemplation of a spiritual or religious truth, the meditator is to develop a sense of heightened religious devotion called forth by his increased awareness of and participation in the reality of the spiritual world. Successful attainment of this goal depends upon the co-ordinated interaction of the imagination or memory, by which the object of the meditation is perceived; the understanding, which provides a rational interpretation and analysis of the object; and the affective faculty, the source of feelings and emotions which are to motivate the soul to action. Following this pattern, the individual meditations of Loyola's *Spiritual Exercises,* after a brief preparatory prayer, usually consist of a tripartite sequence, which Martz designates as composition, analysis, and colloquy.[5] Attempts to recreate the meditative act in poetry or to adapt the methods of meditation to poetry should reflect a part or all of this sequence, taking the form of a peculiar kind of imaginative opening, reflection, and emotional response, respectively.

A concretely conceived image, produced by the power of the imagination or of the memory, is considered a necessary prerequisite to a successful meditation. The first Ignatian exercise, for example, suggests two preludes, one of which involves the "composition of place, seeing the spot," according to which "in contemplation or meditation on visible matters, such as the contemplation of Christ our Lord, who is visible, the composition will be to see with the eyes of the imagination the corporeal place where the thing I wish to contemplate is found."[6] Other practitioners, too, make clear the importance of elaborate and exact detail in the opening image of a meditation. Equally vivid and carefully documented images result from the alternative opening by "placing one-

5. *The Poetry of Meditation,* p. 38. Corresponding to these and indicating the sequence of movement within the meditation are the "three powers of the soul," the acts of memory, understanding, and will. See pp. 34–37.

6. *The Spiritual Exercises of St. Ignatius Loyola. Spanish and English,* ed. Joseph Rickaby, S.J. (London, 1923), p. 23.

self at the spot," that is, by imagining oneself to be at the place which is to be meditated upon, or by actually assuming the identity of the person who is to serve as the subject of the meditation. Thus, the English Jesuit Gibbon suggests that reading about the place, noting the distances there between places and things, the heights of mountains, the location of towns and villages, are all aids to successful meditation.[7] Even in the contemplation of invisible things, a vivid and concrete setting is to be furnished, as in the meditation of sin, where "the composition will be to see with the eyes of the imagination and to consider that my soul is imprisoned within this corruptible body."[8] Martz feels that just such practice of composition is the source of the startlingly direct and graphic openings of many poems by John Donne and George Herbert, where a single moment is presented with dramatic vividness as it apparently passes directly before the poet's eyes, often creating an illusion of colloquial familiarity. Such well-known opening verses as those of Herbert's "The Collar" may serve as an example:

> I struck the board, and cry'd, No more.
>   I will abroad.

The same abrupt quality and air of unexpected familiarity appear in many of Donne's sonnets:

> What if this present were the world's last night?
> Thou hast made me, And shall thy worke decay?

Most striking, perhaps, for its introduction—or lack of it—is Donne's Holy Sonnet 11, which develops from the dramatic depiction of a scene in which the poet imagines himself to suffer the death of Christ:

> Spit in my face, you Jewes, and peirce my side,
> Buffet, and scoffe, scourge, and crucify me,
> For I have sinn'd, and sinn'd, and onely hee,
> Who could do no iniquitie hath dyed:[9]

7. Martz, p. 27.
8. *The Text of the Spiritual Exercises of Saint Ignatius, Translated from the Original Spanish,* 4th ed., with preface by John Morris (Westminster, Md., 1943), p. 20; cited in Martz, p. 28.
9. *The Complete Poetry and Selected Prose of John Donne,* ed. with an introduction by Charles M. Coffin (New York, 1952), pp. 251–52.

When we turn to Gryphius, we find a technique so similar in the opening lines of many sonnets and a general development in others so much like the pattern of a formal meditation that we cannot dismiss, out of hand, the possibility that Gryphius did indeed fashion these poems with an eye toward such devotional exercises. Let us consider as an example the first quartet of the sonnet "An den am Kreutz aufgehenkten Heyland" ("On the Crucified Saviour"):

> Hier wil Ich gantz nicht weg: Laß alle Schwerter klingen /
> Setz Spiß und Sebel an / brauch aller Waffen macht /
> Brauch Fewr / und was die Welt für unerträglich acht /
> Mich soll von Christi Creutz kein Todt noch Teuffel dringen.
> (Werke 1: 6)

> ( I will not leave this spot; draw all your clattering swords,
> Put to me pike and sabre, use all your force of arms,
> Use flame, use torture past enduring—to no avail,
> From Jesus' cross can neither death nor devil force me.)

The suddenness with which the poem begins, as well as the intensity of imagery and tone, which lend the unmistakable impression of a deep and direct personal involvement, are strongly reminiscent of the effect obtained by John Donne from using the method of composition by "placing oneself at the spot." The poem is, in fact, Gryphius' translation of a sonnet by the Jesuit Sarbiewski. His affinity for the poetry of the Jesuits, long a matter of record, is carefully summarized and documented in a recent article by Max Wehrli, "Andreas Gryphius und die Dichtung der Jesuiten."[10] In discussing the poet's imagery, Wehrli points out, though in a completely different context, that in the "Kirchhofsgedanken" Gryphius extends into the realms of hearing and smell those sensations which in Jacob Balde's original are optical alone. Wehrli's comment brings to mind the Ignatian "application of the senses" to meditation. The principle that works to give such an irregular form to so curious a sonnet as "Die Holle" ("Hell"), a poem frequently anthologized as an oddity and cited as an example of Baroque excess, may become clearer (1) when this "application of senses" is suggested for a meditation on hell in the following terms:

10. *Stimmen der Zeit* 90, no. 1 (1964): 25–39.

The first point will be to see those great fires, and those souls as it were in bodies of fire.

The second to hear with the ears lamentations, howlings, cries, blasphemies against Christ.

The third, with the sense of smell, to smell smoke, brimstone, refuse, and rottenness.

The fourth, to taste with the taste bitter things, as tears, sadness, and the worm of conscience.

The fifth, to feel with the sense of touch how those fires do touch and burn souls.

and (2) when this sonnet is considered together with the prelude that precedes this exercise, in which the exercitant shall ask for what he desires of God in the following manner:

. . . it will be here to ask for an intimate sense of the pain that the damned suffer, so that, if through my faults I become forgetful of the love of the Eternal Lord, at least the fear of pain and penalties may be an aid to me not to give way to sin.[11]

No mere exercise in rhetoric or intentional mishandling of the sonnet form without reason, it is rather an attempt to express in poetic terms a meditation on hell by applying to that meditation the means, methods, and form of poetry. The result should be the transformation of a religious devotion into a work of art—or, perhaps more accurately, a fusion of the two:

Ach! und weh!
Mord! Zetter! Jammer! Angst! Creutz! Marter! Würme!
[Plagen.
Pech! Folter! Hencker! Flamm! stanck! Geister! kälte! Zagen!
Ach! vergeh!
Tieff' und Höh'!
Meer! Hügel! Berge! Felß! wer kan die Pein ertragen?
Schluck abgrund! ach schluck' eyn! die nichts denn ewig
[klagen.
Je und Eh!
Schreckliche Geister der tunckelen hölen / Ihr die ihr
[martert und Marter erduldet
Kan denn der ewigen Ewigkeit Fewer / nimmermehr büssen
[dis was ihr verschuldet?

11. P. 41.

O grausamm' Angst / stets sterben sonder sterben /
Diß ist die Flamme der grimmigen Rache / die der erhitzete
[Zorn angeblasen:
Hier ist der Fluch der unendlichen Straffe; hier ist das
[immerdar wachsende rasen:
O Mensch! Verdirb / umb hier nicht zuverderben.
(*Werke* 1: 91)


(Moans and pain!
Murder! Screams! Affliction! Woe! Anguish! Torture!
[Worms! Torment!
Pitch! Hangman! Spirits! Flames! Stench! Rack! Cold!
[Quaking!
O, pass from sight!
Depths and heights!
Swallow up, o abyss, devour those eternally wailing their
[plaints!
Now and forever!
Hideous spirits abiding in darkness, minist'ring torture
[though suff'ring the same,
Can then eternity's undying flames never atone for what you
[have committed?
O horrible anguish! to always be dying, yet never expire!
These are the fires of His furious vengeance, kindled to life
[by His heated wrath!
Here see the curse of an eternal sentence; this is the fury
[that ever increases.
O mortal! perish to yourself in life, that you need not perish
[after death!)


In the octet the application of the senses as an aid to the method of composition by "seeing the spot" or "placing oneself at the spot" produces the powerful immediacy of a vision that can be expressed only in an apparently uncontrollable torrent of agonized gasps, tormented exclamations, and anguished cries of revulsion and dread at the nightmarish suffering perceived. So complete is the speaker's involvement in this scene of ultimate retribution and so immense the horror of the situation that passes before his mind's eye that the depiction of the misery and the tortures all but refuses to be contained by this strictest and most demanding of poetic forms. Composed chiefly of emotional exclamations in what appears to be a random sequence of sense impressions, the sonnet octave remains recognizable as such only by the recurrent end-rhyme. No complete thoughts are presented; rather, the fragmented glimpses of a stunned observer fairly hurtle into their linguistic formulation. The jarring volley of single words and harsh sounds with which this sonnet explodes, rather than begins; the clash of overly long with overly short verses; the thunderous, sharply accented rhythm, in which the unaccented syllables are all but lost completely; and the implied temporary loss of the poet's power to restrain and order—all combine to threaten the very form of the sonnet. Thus it almost seems that the utter negation of human existence which is hell can find expression only in the corresponding negation of that artistic form which was to realize it poetically.

The separation between octet and sestet is especially clearly delineated by the radical changes in meter, rhythm, and syntax, as well as by the reflective quality of lines nine through thirteen, which sets them off sharply from the series of emotional outbursts that comprises the preceding eight lines. After the representation of the subject for the meditation has been completed in the octet, the first two lines of the sestet begin explicitly that act of analysis which forms the second part of a meditation, guided by the second "power of the soul," the understanding. Here the exercitant is to consider and comprehend "by reasoning" the significance of what he has imaginatively perceived by means of the senses during the composition. While there is certainly no hint of inner calm in the galloping dactyls of the sestet, there is a smoothness to the flow of rhythm that reflects a balance and ordering power of the rational process, which is not present in the first eight lines. The third "power of the soul," the will, concludes the sonnet with a colloquy in the form of an exhortation directed simultaneously to the self and to every sinner: "O Mensch! Verdirb / umb hier nicht zuverderben."

"Die Hölle" is by no means an isolated example of the way in which the methods and the general tenor of the practice of meditation may have been assimilated into Gryphius' poetry. In fact, it is itself one of a series of five poems that close the second book of sonnets, all of which correspond to certain frequently found topics of formal meditation. It is the third of four poems which, together, could very well constitute an extended meditation on the "last things," a sequence suggested by Loyola, St. Francis de Sales, Fray Luis de Granada, and others. The goal of this sequence is the at-

tainment of that degree of self-knowledge which will permit the individual to turn from a life of sin and corruption to one of contemplation and love of God. Such meditations as these in particular
serve to evoke emotions of fear and horror, emotions which a later
writer working in the same tradition calls "profitably terrible,"
since they stimulate the soul to increased religious devotion.[12] Although not all the poems of this group display with equal clarity
that three-part structure of composition, analysis, and colloquy
which we have noted in "Die Hölle," each one does exhibit unmis-
takably one or more of the elements of the formal meditation. Like
that on hell, the meditation on the Last Judgment opens with a
vividly direct composition of place:

Das Letzte Gerichte
(The Last Judgment)

Auff Todten! auff! die welt verkracht in letztem brande!
   Der Sternen Heer vergeht! der Mond ist dunckel-rott /
   Die Sonn' ohn allen schein! Auff / Ihr die grab und kott
Auff! ihr die Erd und See und Hellen hilt zu pfande!
   Ihr die ihr lebt komm't an: der HERR / der vor in schande
   Sich richten ließ / erscheint / vor Ihm laufft flamm' und noth
Bey Ihm steht Majestätt / nach ihm / folgt blitz und todt /
   Umb ihn / mehr Cherubim als Sand an Pontus strande.
Wie lieblich spricht Er an / die seine Recht' erkohren.
Wie schrecklich donnert Er / auff diese die verlohren
   Unwiderrufflich wortt / kommt Freunde! Feinde fliht'
Der Himmel schleußt sich auff! O Gott! welch frölich
                            [scheiden!
Die Erden reist entzwey. Welch weh / welch schrecklich
                             [leiden.
   Weh / weh dem / der verdamm't: wol dem der IESUM
                             [siht.

(Werke 1: 90)

(Rise, O dead, rise! The world collapses in final fiery agony!
The stars' bright troop must yield; the moon shines darkly
                             [red,

---

12. James Hervey, "Meditations Among the Tombs," in *The Whole
Works of the Late Reverend James Hervey, A.M. in Six Volumes,* vol. 1
(Edinburgh, 1802), p. 111.

The sun has lost its radiance. Rise! you whom grave and
[dirt,
You whom earth and sea and Hell itself hold hostage!
You who are the living, come, come! The Lord, who once in
[shame
Gave Himself to be judged, appears. Before Him flickers flame
[and distress,
With Him stands majesty, behind march lightning and death,
About Him more cherubs than sand on Pontus' shores.
How lovingly He speaks to those who chose His laws!
How fearfully He thunders His awful final words
At those who have not heeded: Come, friends! My enemies,
[flee!
The Heavens separate! O Lord, what joyous parting!
The earth is rent! What misery, what frightful suffering!
Woe, woe to him who is damned! Blessed be he who sees
[Lord Jesus!)

Although the imaginative faculty dominates in this sonnet, after a visualization of the turmoil and upheavals in the natural world as they are predicted for this last day in the Scriptures, the understanding does begin an analysis of the causes and circumstances of the situation. The sonnet closes with a colloquy which can only be taken as an admonition to those now living to seek to avoid the fate of the damned while there is yet time.

Even more dramatic and direct are the results of the composition of place in "Ewige Frewde der Außerwehlten" ("Eternal Joy of the Chosen"), the sonnet directly following "Die Hölle," in which the poet assumes the identity of one of the elect. The poem opens with the words of the suddenly awakening soul in a state of confusion and astonished disbelief:

O! wo bin ich! O was seh' ich! wach ich! treumt mir? wie
[wird mir
JESU! welcher wollust Meer / überschwemmt mein
[frölich Hertz /
Welt Ade! glück zu mein trost! gutte Nacht todt angst
[und schmertz /
Ich find alles, alles lern ich! alles schaw' ich HERR in dir
Ich zuschmeltz in lautter wonne! JESu: JESu. meine zier!
O wie herrlich ists hier seyn! Erde deine Frewd ist
[schertz!

JESu! ewig-gläntzend Licht' (tunckel ist der Sonnen
[kertz!)
Ach! wie funckeln deine Scharen! Sternen fliht! hier
[schimmern wir.
Ihr die ihr glutt und Schwerd verlacht! ob schon ewr Leib
[wurd staub und aschen /
Ihr die ihr ewer reines kleid habt in dem Blutt deß Lambs
[gewaschen /
Rufft Halleluja! Halleluja! frewd und leben!
Dir dreymal einig Ewigkeit; die alles in allen allmächtig
[regiret:
Sey unaußprechlich Lob und ruhm / und Ehre die dir nur
[alleine gebühret.
Dir / die sich ewig / (Halleluja!) uns wil geben.
(*Werke* 1: 91–92)


(Oh, where am I! What vision here? waking? dreaming?
[how should I tell?
Jesus! how sweet the sea of pleasure engulfing my happy
[heart!
Farewell, world! I hasten, my consolation! good night, death,
[fear, and pain!
All things I find, all things I learn, all things I glimpse in
[Thee, Lord.
In pure bliss I dissolve! Jesus, Jesus, my precious jewel!
Oh, how glorious to be here! Earth, Thy pleasure is but
[chaff!
Jesus! constant shining light (how dark by contrast the sun's
[bright flame!)
O, how bright your satellites do sparkle! Stars, be gone, 'tis
[we who glitter here!
Oh you who scorned both flames and sword, though your
[flesh was turned to dust and ashes,
You who have washed your habit pure in blood of the sacred
[lamb,
Shout halleluja, halleluja, joy and life!
Thou eternal trinity, almighty ruler of all things,
May Thine be praise beyond expression, and honor befitting
[Thee alone.
To Thee who gives Thyself to us, we sing halleluja!)


However, now that the goal of its journey is achieved, the attainment of the soul to the realm of pure spirit is represented in lan-

guage which is almost entirely spiritual; language is converted into a vehicle for expressing almost solely the emotions. The imagination, unable to describe in concrete images a scene or events which can be perceived through the senses, turns inward in an attempted description of the overwhelming bliss of the fortunate soul which has been saved. The imagination has here reached that mystical level where it sees simultaneously everything and nothing. The soul proclaims "alles schaw' ich," but it tells of seeing nothing but light. The reasoning mind, too, achieves complete knowledge: "Ich find alles, alles lern ich," but in the attempt to analyze and express the salient features of this spiritual union, it is thrown back upon vague traditional comparisons such as those of lines seven and eight. The religious phrases and metaphors, the language of mysticism as used in lines two and five, denote little, but connote the spiritual state of joy. For the benefits received, the soul, in the colloquy, calls for thanks and praise which must remain indeed "unaußprechlich."

In his article "Two Quartets: Sonnet Cycles by Andreas Gryphius," to which reference was made above, de Capua reminds us that the same book of sonnets, which closes with the cycle of four just now discussed, also opens with a quartet, the four time-of-day sonnets. Although clearly intended as an integrated cycle by the author, they, too, he points out, have never been so considered in the critical literature. Indeed, even in the penetrating analyses to which these four poems are submitted by Jöns, because of the external plan of his book and the point he wishes to make, they are not treated really as members of a connected cycle, and the closeness of their interrelationship is necessarily de-emphasized.[13] The external basis for their interdependence could lie in the fact that the sonnets are either intended as or patterned after an extended meditation on time, death, and eternity. Jöns' thorough discussion of Gryphius' use in these poems of the analogical method, amply documented, well-presented, and convincing as it is, needs no further comment. What should be stressed somewhat more, however, is that the four work simultaneously on three different levels: man's *Lebenstag*, the duration of the existence of the created universe, and the single twenty-four-hour day during which this meditation takes place. The last of these three levels, announced by the titles of the individual sonnets, is at once the most obvious and the

13. See *Das "Sinnen-Bild,"* pp. 91 ff., 167–83.

most neglected. The swiftness with which this day passes brings
the meditating soul to a realization of the imminence of death, the
rapidly approaching end of creation, and the certainty of final
judgment. These insights, a primary goal of this meditation, are
presented in increasingly longer and more detailed sections throughout the course of the quartet—in "Morgen," lines 13–14; "Mittag,"
12–14; "Abend," 6–7 and 12–14; and "Mitternacht," 9–14:

I

Morgen Sonnet
(Morning Sonnet)

DIe ewig helle schar wil nun jhr licht verschlissen /
　　Diane steht erblaßt; die Morgenrötte lacht
　　Den grawen Himmel an / der sanffte Wind erwacht /
Vnd reitzt das Federvolck / den newen Tag zu grüssen.
Das leben dieser welt / eilt schon die welt zu küssen /
　　Vnd steckt sein Haupt empor / man siht der Stralen pracht
　　Nun blinckern auf der See: O dreymal höchste Macht
Erleuchte den / der sich jtzt beugt vor deinen Füssen.
　　Vertreib die dicke Nacht / die meine Seel vmbgibt /
　　Die Schmertzen Finsternüß die Hertz vnd geist betrübt /
Erquicke mein gemüt / vnd stärcke mein vertrawen.
　　Gib / daß ich diesen Tag / in deinem dinst allein
　　Zubring; vnd wenn mein End' vnd jener Tag bricht ein
Daß ich dich meine Sonn / mein Licht mög ewig schawen.
　　　　　　　　　　　　　　　　　　(Werke 1: 65)

(The endless-shining troop will now its light conceal.
Diana stands all pale; Dawn's blushing smile sends rays
Upon the greyish sky; a gentle breeze is stirring
And prods the winged songsters to hail the newborn day.
The dwellers of this world make haste that world to greet
And strain to raise their heads to catch its golden splendor
Now gleaming on the bay. O mighty force above,
Shine down on him who kneels before your feet!
Drive out the heavy night that holds my soul in bondage,
The gloominess of pain that darkens heart and mind!
Restore my weary spirit, make strong my faith!
Allow me this one day at your command alone
To serve! And when that day arrives that marks my end,
Then grant, my sun, my light, eternal sight of you.)

## II

### Mittag
### (Noon)

AUff Freunde! last vnß zu der Taffel eylen /
  In dem die Sonn ins Himmels mittel hält
  Vnd der von Hitz vnd arbeit matten Welt
Sucht jhren weg / vnd vnsern Tag zu theilen.
Der Blumen Zier wird von den flammen pfeylen
  Zu hart versehrt / das außgedörtte Feldt
  Wündscht nach dem Taw' der schnitter nach dem zelt
Kein Vogel klagt von seinen Liebes seilen.
  Das Licht regiert / der schwartze Schatten fleucht
  In eine höl / in welche sich verkreucht
Den Schand vnd furcht sich zu verbergen zwinget.
  Man kan dem glantz des tages ja entgehn!
  Doch nicht dem licht / daß / wo wir immer stehn /
Vns siht vnd richt / vnd hell' vnd grufft durch dringet.

(Werke 1: 65–66)

(Come, friends! let us hurry to the waiting table,
While the sun still holds its midpoint in the Heavens
And, for a world weak from heat and toil,
Seeks to part its course and our day!
The flowers' blossoms, struck by flaming darts,
Are too severely scorched, the withered field
Yearns for the vanished dew, the reaper for his tent;
No bird gives voice to plaints of love's sweet bondage.
Now light prevails; the somber shadows fly
Into a cavern, in which there now takes refuge
He whom shame and fear have forced to hide.
One can indeed escape the light of day,
But not that light which, where'er we stand,
Can see and judge, pierce Hell and grave as well.)

## III

### Abend
### (Evening)

DEr schnelle Tag ist hin / die Nacht schwingt jhre fahn /
Vnd führt die Sternen auff. Der Menschen müde scharen
Verlassen feld vnd werck / Wo Thier vnd Vögel waren

Trawrt jtzt die Einsamkeit. Wie ist die zeit verthan!
Der port naht mehr vnd mehr sich / zu der glieder Kahn.
Gleich wie diß licht verfiel / so wird in wenig Jahren
Ich / du / vnd was man hat / vnd was man siht / hinfahren.
Diß Leben kömmt mir vor alß eine renne bahn.
Laß höchster Gott mich doch nicht auff dem Laufplatz gleiten /
Laß mich nicht ach / nicht pracht / nicht lust / nicht angst
[verleiten.
Dein ewig heller glantz sey vor vnd neben mir /
Laß / wenn der müde Leib entschläfft / die Seele wachen
Vnd wenn der letzte Tag wird mit mir abend machen /
So reiß mich auß dem thal der Finsternuß zu Dir.

(*Werke* 1: 66)
(already translated on pp. 68–69)


IV

Mitternacht
(Midnight)

SChrecken / vnd stille / vnd dunckeles grausen / finstere
[kälte bedecket das Land /
Jtzt schläfft was arbeit vnd schmertzen ermüdet / diß sind
[der trawrigen einsamkeit stunden.
Nunmehr ist / was durch die Lüffte sich reget / nunmehr
[sind Thiere vnd Menschen verschwunden.
Ob zwar die jmmerdar schimmernde lichter / der ewig
[schitternden Sternen entbrand!
Suchet ein fleißiger Sinn noch zu wachen? der durch
[bemühung der künstlichen hand /
Ihm die auch nach vns ankommende Seelen / Ihm / die an
[jtzt sich hier finden verbunden?
Wetztet ein bluttiger Mörder die Klinge? wil er unschuldiger
[Hertzen verwunden?
Sorget ein ehren-begehrende Seele / wie zuerlangen ein
[höherer stand?
Sterbliche! Sterbliche! lasset diß dichten! Morgen! ach!
[morgen ach! muß man hin zihn!
Ach wir verschwinden gleich alß die gespenste / die vmb
[die stund unß erscheinen vnd flihn.
Wenn vnß die finstere gruben bedecket / wird was wir
[wündschen vnd suchen zu nichte.
Doch wie der gläntzende Morgen eröffnet / was weder
[Monde noch Fackel bescheint:

So wenn der plötzliche Tag wird anbrechen / wird was
[geredet / gewürcket / gemeynt.
Sonder vermänteln eröffnet sich finden vor deß
[erschrecklichen GOttes Gerichte.
(*Werke* 1: 67)

(Terror and silence and ebony horror, gloomy frigidness
[covers the land.
Now sleep those weary from labors and pain, these are the
[hours of sorrowful loneliness.
Gone are the wings that once stirred the air, gone are the
[animals, vanished the people.
Although the eternally flickering lamps of ceaselessly
[glistening stars are aglow,
Is there a diligent mind still at work, which, through the arts
[of a competent hand,
Binds itself now to those souls who'll come after and to those
[who now inhabit this earth?
Do blood-thirsty murderers whet now their weapons? Will
[they cut through a quite innocent heart?
Are there still waking hearts gnawed by ambition, worrying
[how to reach higher distinctions?
Mortals, O mortals, abandon such fancies! Already tomorrow
[perhaps you must die!
Alas, we must vanish just as do those spirits who, at that
[hour, appear and then fly!
When we are decked by the grave's gloomy darkness, then
[what we yearn for and strive for is naught.
But, just as the sun-streaks of morning disclose what neither
[the moonlight nor lanterns make clear,
So when that sudden Last Day comes upon us, all we have
[said, intended, accomplished
Shall be laid bare of protective devices and placed before
[that most fearful court's judge.)

In addition to the evident temporal relationship between the sonnets, consisting of the linear movement from morning to midnight,
they are connected also in a pair-wise, nonlinear linking by a variety of formal relationships, especially parallels and contrasts.
Thus "Morgen" and "Abend" are linked by their closing prayers,
which may suggest the religious practice of performing morning
and evening devotions at these pivotal points of the twenty-four-
hour day. Similarly, in addition to the play of light and darkness,

and of "Tag"/"Abend," "Leben"/"Lebensende," which is central to all four poems, the first and third sonnets share an unusual number of words in common—"Schar," "ewig-hell," "Seele," "Finsternis," and "und wenn," which also introduces the same idea, at the same position, line thirteen, in each sonnet. Through an oblique association, which is nevertheless readily recognizable, a common image begins both the sonnets, too: the personified stars of "Abend," represented as a troop of soldiers, recall "DIe ewig helle schar" of "Morgen," line one, also a metaphor for the stars. Both poems are written in alexandrines with masculine and feminine rhymes, but "Abend" has masculine rhymes where "Morgen" has feminine, and feminine rhymes in those lines where "Morgen" has masculine, suggesting, perhaps, that, despite the physical similarities between these two significant times, morning and evening do stand at opposite ends of the day.

If the poetic "I" of "Morgen" and "Abend," introduced in each in the second quatrain, leads to the prayer of the sestets, it appears also in "Mittag" and "Mitternacht," projecting itself physically in the first line of the former, where it becomes an actor in a poem marked by activity, but spiritually in "Mitternacht," where all external activity has ceased. In this latter sonnet, peering into the surrounding darkness, it perceives its own feelings. Both poems conclude with an admonition rather than a prayer, but both are also connected by the contrasts of light and darkness, heat and cold, activity and stillness, a natural world which is conceived in optical images and a scene removed inward, in which emotions and thoughts replace sense perceptions. Metrically, "Mittag" is written in unusually short, five-foot lines of relatively calm and stable iambs, while "Mitternacht" is composed in unusually long, eight-foot lines of rushing dactyls. The masculine-feminine rhyme patterns of the two poems, opposed in the octets, are alike in the sestets, as an indication, perhaps, that antitheses meet at the extremes.

If the play of light and darkness dominates the cycle, the opening sonnet "Morgen" is completely suffused by positive bright light and the animated life which it calls forth and sustains. However, the ever-increasing darkness, literal and figurative, which gradually comes to prevail in the following three sonnets, is already present here, at least as a presentiment. In contrast to the fresh vivacity of the natural world, which is eager to greet the new day, stands man's spiritual weariness, of which the sestet's prayer is born and which increases as the sonnet cycle—and the concrete day of meditation—progresses. Nature need utter no plea for *Erquickung*—its joyful innocence and readiness to react and come alive are evident and spontaneous; not so man, who is already spiritually ill. The prayer is one for grace, and already with "jener Tag" of line thirteen, which recurs as "der plötzliche Tag" in the parallel line of "Mitternacht" with a stronger sense of impending doom, there is a hint of the eschatological terrors which lurk behind the entire meditation, but which are realized fully only when the imminence and inevitability of that Day of Judgment occupy the central position in a meditating mind which recognizes that time is running out.

In "Mittag" the forced conviviality of the opening lines dissolves in the second quartet and cannot obscure the fact that the same Divine light which pervades "Morgen" can be an outright threat, filling man with fear rather than affording solace. The sun is a threat not only because of the destruction wrought by its rays, but also because, from this point of its zenith at noon, it can only move downward, toward darkness and the end of the day of meditation, where the meditator must take stock of his spiritual gains. The meditation continues in "Abend," but the hope of "Morgen" now seems even more to have been in vain, for the day has progressed all too quickly and now moves rapidly toward its end. Man's activities in this world, because they are of this world, count as nothing. His labors in the fields are certainly of no consequence. A sense of the helplessness and almost hopelessness of his lot deepens here, and if the prayer of "Morgen" reflects a mild though growing spiritual disquiet, that of "Abend" is born of near-desperation. But only in the thundering octameters of "Mitternacht," whose tempo mirrors the uncontrollable speed with which the day now seems to rush to its conclusion, are the flood gates fully open. The mounting fears have reached their peak. Far from attaining that peace of mind which is the real goal of such a meditation and is to stem from the insights gained, the poetic "I" concludes, vastly more agitated than when it began the sequence, in contemplation of the horrors waiting at "GOttes Gerichte." The day of meditation has, in fact, succeeded only partially. The insights into his spiritual condition and into the necessary result of such a condition have failed to turn the speaker of the poems toward the Divine. The grace requested in "Morgen" and pleaded for in "Abend" does not seem to have come, and he must move on to a new day and a new attempt.

Elsewhere Gryphius pleads for time, for a few years free of oppression, misery, and fear:

Schluß des 1648 sten Jahres<br>
(On the End of the Year 1648)

Zeuch hin betrübtes Jahr / zeuch hin mit meinen Schmertzen!
   Zeuch hin mit meiner Angst und überhäufften Weh!
   Zeuch so viel Leichen nach! Bedrängte Zeit vergeh /
Und führe mit dir weg die Last von diesem Hertzen!
HErr / vor dem unser Jahr als ein Geschwätz und Schertzen /
   Fällt meine Zeit nicht hin wie ein verschmeltzter Schnee /
   Laß doch / weil mir die Sonn gleich in der Mittags-Höh /
Mich noch nicht untergehn / gleich ausgebrennten Kertzen.
   HErr es ist genung geschlagen /
   Angst und Ach genung getragen /
Gib doch nun etwas Frist / daß ich mich recht bedencke /
   Gib daß ich der Handvoll Jahre
   Froh werd' eins vor meiner Bahre /
Mißgönne mir doch nicht dein liebliches Geschencke.
(Werke 1: 103)

(Move on, O year of gloom, move on with all my pain!
Move on with all my fears and misery heaped on high!
Move on, follow the corpses! Oppressive time, pass on,
And lead away with you the burden from this heart!
Lord, to whom our years are merely idle chatter,
Do not let my time pass like melted snow in spring,
But grant, while my sun stands at the zenith of midday,
That I do not yet perish like a blackened, burned-out taper.
Lord, I have enough of blows,
Endured enough of fear and woe,
Allow me some slight time in which to set my thoughts aright.
Grant that of my handful of years,
One shall give me joy before my bier.
How can You fail to grant this loving gift to me?)

It is not, as it may first seem, a plea for a few years of pleasure in the enjoyment of life, but a prayer for time for spiritual preparation, "daß ich mich recht bedencke," before the last day of life, which is also the last day before *Jüngstes Gericht*. Clearly, contemplation of the terrors awaiting an unredeemed soul are not sufficient, and it may well be that what Gryphius strives for is to move beyond attrition, a stage which he has evidently already reached, to true contrition out of love of God, not fear, as the two are distinguished in the Anglican church.[14] If so, it remains as a goal after "Mitternacht." Jöns is certainly correct in his interpretation of "Mitternacht" and in his explication of the key line, four. We are, in fact, returned once again to the state of affairs and the state of the soul described in the first chapter of this book, for in "Mitternacht" no less than in "Es ist alles eitell," the poet most certainly includes himself among those admonished in the sestet.

Despite general similarities of purpose and form, the sonnet "Einsambkeit" ("Solitude") is quite different in certain respects from the type of meditative poem we have been considering until now. Rather than being simply a meditation itself, this sonnet presents the poet following in his mind and describing the process of a specific act of meditation. It is a poem about meditation, written by a meditator who has "arrived," not at any kind of mystical union, but at a degree of self-knowledge and understanding of the relationship between man and the Divine which leads in turn to that condition of spiritual well-being which the practice of meditation should afford the faithful practitioner:

IN dieser Einsambkeit / der mehr denn öden wüsten /
  Gestreckt auff wildes Kraut / an die bemößte See:
  Beschaw' ich jenes Thal und dieser Felsen höh'
Auff welchem Eulen nur und stille Vögel nisten.
Hier fern von dem Pallast; weit von deß Pövels lüsten /
  Betracht ich: wie der Mensch in Eitelkeit vergeh'
  Wie auff nicht festem grund' all unser hoffen steh'
Wie die vor abend schmähn / die vor dem tag unß grüßten.
  Die Höell / der rawe wald / der Todtenkopff / der Stein /
  Den auch die zeit aufffrist / die abgezehrten bein.
Entwerffen in dem Mut unzehliche gedancken.
  Der Mauren alter grauß / diß ungebaw'te Land
  Ist schön und fruchtbar mir / der eigentlich erkant /
Das alles / ohn ein Geist / den GOt selbst hält / muß wacken.

                           (*Werke* 1: 68)

14. For an interesting study of this subject in connection with Donne's poetry, see Douglas L. Peterson, "John Donne's *Holy Sonnets* and the Anglican Doctrine of Contrition," *Studies in Philology* 56 (1959), 504–18.

(In this solitude of desolate waste-land,
Resting on the grass grown wild along the mossy sea,
I look upon that vale and on those rocky heights
Where only owls and silent birds remain.
Here, as far from wealthy courts as from the joys of poorer
                                      [men,
I contemplate how man must fade away in vanity,
How all our hopes are built on shifting sands,
How kindly morning greetings may turn to evening scorn.
This cave, the wild forest, the ivory skull, the stone,
Devoured too by time, the fleshless unknown bones,
All these have filled my mind with countless thoughts.
The gloom of these old walls, the uncultivated land,
Holds beauty and great value for one like me who knows
That no soul can sustain itself without a life in God.)

Pervaded by an atmosphere of calm and tranquility, the sonnet is formed and controlled by the reflections of a speaker who stands above the experience and reports on the progress of the meditation in an unusually detached manner.[15] Although the description of the first four lines is concrete and specific, there is no trace here, or anywhere else in the poem, of those direct and sudden outpourings of emotion that we have noted in the sonnets discussed above. That the octet is the account of the course of composition and analysis in meditation is underscored by the use of the verbs "beschauen" and "betrachten," which refer respectively to the image-forming and reflective faculties. The thoughts of lines six through eight, varied as are the elements of the landscape in lines nine and ten which provoke them, are all concerned with man's situation in this world. The considerations of the vanity and transience of human life, the insecure foundations upon which man's aspirations rest, and the inconstancy of seeming friends are all linked by the underlying theme of the instability of human existence and the resulting weakness of man's position.

    15. Powell is correct in his estimation of Gryphius' relationship to nature, of which this poem is seen as an example: "The poet does not feel at one with Nature; he stands aloof and *reflects.*" *Andreas Gryphius, Carolus Stuardus,* ed. Hugh Powell (Leicester, 1955), p. lvii. The same sort of objective detachment, however, is found in several poems in which the poet contemplates the disintegration of his own body. In both situations it would seem to reflect the state of meditation. Cf. Martz, p. 130, on the source of the speaker's power of detachment in meditative poetry.

In the sestet the "affective" faculty of the soul is not stimulated in the customary way to make an emotional response in the form of colloquy or prayer to the ideas developed above; instead, the emotions are restrained by the reasoning mind, which continues to order the experiences of the senses.[16] These last six lines are devoted to an enumeration of the individual objects discerned in the scene described by the first quartet, and, in very general terms, to a statement of the results and the value of the meditation. If we stay within the context of the sonnet, then we must conclude that, contrary to the interpretation by Jöns, the "unzehliche gedancken" of line eleven refer quite clearly to that variety of thoughts indicated, in part, in lines six through eight.[17] Just as the poet selects for us, apparently at random, only some of the objects from the landscape which stimulate these thoughts, so, too, the thoughts themselves which appear in the octet represent merely a random sampling that is by no means complete here. Surely "unzehliche" here carries the meaning of "countless" in the sense of extremely numerous, rather than literally "infinite" or "inexhaustible," as Jöns would have it. Furthermore, Jöns may be correct in his feeling that to consider this section of the sonnet as a reflection on transience alone is to view it too narrowly; however, his own interpretation of the poem, for which the meaning of lines eleven and fourteen and the role of nature in the sestet are decisive, is itself open to question. No one can argue the validity of his general statements concerning the seventeenth-century poets' view of nature and the function often served by the depiction of the natural

16. This "ordering" process is visible, too, in the formal construction of the poem. Through the presentation of a catalog of disconnected nature images, the sestet emphasizes the lack of order in the landscape as well as an aura of decay. Thus an originally cohesive landscape disintegrates and the components of the natural world become a series of emblems for transience. This discontinuity and lack of order is further expressed structurally by the division of natural description into three sections, lines 1–4, 9–10, and 12. Counterbalancing this threat of chaos in nature is the order created by the forming power of the poet, which confronts the seven lines of nature description with seven limiting reflective lines. These two elements balance in the pattern 4–4, 2–1, 1–2, corresponding to the formal sonnet division into octet and tercets.

17. It is possible that the poem is one about meditation, in general, rather than any one specific act of meditation. The "unzehliche Gedancken" could refer to thoughts stimulated by earlier meditations or usually called forth in similar situations in the past. The insight of line fourteen would then be one which was gained before and which now makes spiritual profit possible in any such meditation.

world in their poetry. It is true that for many poets of the Baroque the significance of the phenomena of the natural world lay in their power to reveal or reflect something of the Divine, and the contemplation of nature was a means of recognizing the omnipotence and omnipresence of God. The tradition of Christian allegory and analogy still flourished in the literature. Gryphius, too, often thumbed the pages of the great Book of Nature, from the chapters of which he culled the wisdom that crystallized in his poems as moral insights and teachings. Nevertheless, we cannot accept the application of these ideas to the sonnet "Einsambkeit" in quite the way that Jöns suggests: " 'Entwerffen' die Dinge 'in dem Mutt unzehliche Gedancken,' so bedeutet das die im meditierenden Betrachten vernommene Sprache der Schöpfung, die dem Ich, das 'eigentlich erkannt' hat, daß alles Seiende von der Kraft des Geistes Gottes getragen ist, eine jenseits alles Sichtbaren liegende Wirklichkeit offenbart." ("If these things 'fill the mind with countless thoughts,' the reference is to that language of creation heard during meditative contemplation, which reveals to the 'I,' which itself has already recognized that all existing things are sustained by the power of God's spirit, a reality that lies beyond all that is visible.")[18] After quoting from the *Vier Bycher vom wahren Christentum* several biblical references and comments on them by Arndt, all supporting this idea, Jöns goes on to draw his conclusions about the poem: "Von dieser Grundlage barocken Bibelchristentums aus wird im Sichtbaren und Zeitlichen das Unsichtbare und Ewige, Gott als Schöpfer und Erhalter alles Seienden gesehen, und auf die Betonung dieser Perspektive, die die in ihrer faktischen Beschaffenheit unfruchtbare und dem Auge keine Schönheit bietende Einöde 'schön und fruchtbar' werden läßt, kommt es Gryphius an, wie der in dialektischer Antithetik herausgearbeitete Schluß des Sonetts zeigt." ("From this standpoint of Baroque Christianity, which is firmly rooted in the Bible, the invisible and eternal is seen in the visible and temporal, and God is viewed as the creator and the sustainer of all that exists. Gryphius is concerned with emphasizing this perspective, which causes that desolation, itself in reality unfruitful and offering no beauty to the observing eye, to become 'beautiful and fruitful,' as the conclusion of the sonnet, with its dialectical antithesis, demonstrates.")[19] Jöns' reading of line four-

18. *Das "Sinnen-Bild,"* p. 89.
19. *Das "Sinnen-Bild,"* pp. 89–90.

teen, however, which in combination with his treatment of the rest of the sestet allows such a conclusion, distorts the meaning of the line by shifting the emphasis from one element to another. In his paraphrase of the line, cited above, he forces a syntactical change which effectively reverses the intended meaning, actually transforming the statement into its logical contradictory. Jöns disregards the implication of a negative in this closing *pointe*, which in fact recapitulates the antithesis of lines twelve and thirteen. Only by doing so can he assert that what the poem recognizes is "daß alles Seiende von der Kraft des Geistes Gottes getragen ist," excluding the possibility of the existence of things that do not belong to this category. Yet it is precisely, with such things that Gryphius is clearly reckoning: "Das *alles / ohn ein Geist /* den GOt selbst hält / *muß wancken*" (italics mine). Had Gryphius wished to make such a comment on life as Jöns insists he does, we can speculate that the subjunctive of the modal would have helped his cause. At any rate, as it is, line fourteen is the equivalent of a "real" condition:

Wenn etwas einen Geist hat, den Gott nicht selbst hält, so
[muß es wancken,

which leaves open the possibility that the statement of the "if" clause is true. It is not here a question of the poet's realization of the Divine spirit which permeates everything—the comprehension of a higher reality which transforms the transparent ugliness and lifelessness of the sterile objects he sees into the beauty of the eternal. Rather, the practitioner of meditation recognizes the necessity of achieving a spirit rooted in God, a goal attainable through meditation. In utter desolation, through contemplation of even the morbid and the frightening, of death and decay, the meditator has found material which is beautiful and fruitful for him in its effect on his soul. For the exercitant, the mental concentration on such things and the resulting stimulation of feelings of fear and horror are to lead the mind, by way of the "holy fear" of death and Divine punishment, to the hatred of sin and the love of God, and, ultimately, to sincere contrition. Gryphius speaks elsewhere of true freedom in terms of the "freie Geist":

Waß ist die Freyheit doch / die nirgend wird gefunden /
Du bist eh' als du bist / vnd weil du bist gebunden /

Du bindest dich selb-selbst in Furcht vnd Sorgen eyn.
Doch! wer mit schnellem geist kan durch die Wolcken rennen /
Und stricke / die verlust vnd hoffnung / würckt zutrennen;
  Kan / ob ihn Diamant gleich bünde / freye seyn.
                                    (*Werke* 1: 71)

(But what is that real freedom which is nowhere found?
You are, before you are, and while you are, tight bound.
You bind yourself yourself through worries and through fears.
But he whose swift soul races through the clouds above
And bursts the bonds that both despair and hope have tied,
He can be free, though he be bound by chains of diamond.)

Ade Welt! Gunst Ade! jetzt bin ich nicht mehr dein.
Ich wil den freyen Geist / nun wehmut frey / erheben /
Ich wil mit freyem Sinn / weit vber alle schweben.
  Die stränge dinstbarkeit schleußt in viel ketten eyn!
                                    (*Werke* 1: 72)

(Farewell, world! favor, farewell! now I am no more thine.
My spirit free, of sorrow freed, shall rise now.
High above all I'll soar with my free mind.
Our servitude severe imprisons us with many chains.)

It would seem that the poet here is speaking of the same life of contemplation in meditation and condition of the soul which, in "Einsambkeit," he describes himself as either having reached or actively pursuing.

A few words remain to be said about a relatively recent discussion of the sonnet "Trawrklage des Autoris / in sehr schwerer Kranckheit" ("Lament of the Author during his Severe Illness"). Marian Szyrocki deals with the poem, unhappily in the midst of a biographical sketch of the author. Proceeding from the fact that the date of this poem coincides roughly with the time of the *Fasching* celebration in Danzig, where Gryphius was then living, Szyrocki, in what is his sole significant comment on the sonnet, offers the extraordinary hypothesis that it may have resulted from the poet's overindulgence at *Fasching*:[20]

Ich bin nicht / der ich war / Die kräffte sind verschwunden!
Die Glieder sind verdorrt wie ein verbrandter Grauß /

20. *Der junge Gryphius,* Neue Beiträge zur Literaturwissenschaft, vol. 9 (Berlin, 1959), p. 74.

Hier schawt der schwartze Todt zu beyden Augen auß /
Nichts wird als Haut vnd Bein mehr an mir vbrig funden.
Der Athem wil nicht fort; die Zung steht angebunden.
    Mein Hertz das vbersteht nunmehr den letzten Strauß /
    Ein jeder / der mich siht spürt daß das schwache Hauß
Der Leib wird brechen ein / gar inner wenig Stunden /
    Gleich wie die Wiesenblum früh mit dem Liecht der Welt
    Hervor kombt / vnnd noch eh der Mittag weggeht / fält;
So bin ich auch benetzt mit Thränentaw ankommen:
    So sterb ich vor der Zeit: O Erden gutte Nacht!
    Mein Stündlein laufft herbey! nun hab ich außgewacht /
Und werde von dem Schlaff des Todes eingenommen!
                                        (*Werke* 1: 8)

(I am not what I was. My strength has disappeared!
My limbs are dry and crumbling like a piece of burned-out
                                        [coal.
Look into my eyes and see how death awaits his prey,
Of me now naught remains to see but skin and bone.
My breath has ceased its rhythm; my tongue now moves no
                                        [more.
My heart alone will not concede that final struggle yet.
Who looks at me can plainly see that this weak house,
My body, must, within a few short hours, collapse.
Just as the wild flower early with the light of day
Appears, and yet, before the hour of noon, is dead,
So I have come, shrouded with a dew of tears,
And so I die before my time—oh Earth, farewell!
The hour hand speeds by, now I have waked too long,
And must be carried off by sleep-bestower Death.)

Of course, it may be that this sonnet was occasioned by an actual physical sickness, but the ever-present and unavoidable illness of the soul would have provided reason enough for a meditation on death. Like the meditations on the sins and the "last things," such a preparation for death through contemplation of it would allow the soul to search upward and consider more seriously its own ultimate fate. Because it is impossible to calculate the time of death's arrival, it was to be practiced repeatedly. As St. Francis de Sales remarks in his fifth meditation, *On Death:* "this only is certain that we shall die, and that always sooner than we expect."[21] The salutary

---

21. *Introduction to the Devout Life* (Oxford and Cambridge, 1877), p. 24.

value of keeping the time of one's death constantly in mind, an idea which has its roots perhaps in the medieval *Ars Moriendi* and is further developed by the meditation on death, finds expression elsewhere in Gryphius' poetry. It is clearest in those poems where the "moment" about which the poet is concerned is obviously that of death, as in the epigram "Betrachtung der Zeit":

> Mein sind die Jahre nicht, die mir die Zeit genommen /
> Mein sind die Jahre nicht, die etwa möchten kommen;
> Der Augenblick ist mein, und nehm' ich den in acht,
> So ist der mein, der Jahr und Ewigkeit gemacht.
>
> (*Werke* 2: 182)
> (already translated on p. 43)

Gryphius' seemingly pathological preoccupation with death appears, then, to reflect the influence of the meditation on death, especially in those poems where the mind is apparently able to observe and analyze the decomposition of the body in all its horrifying detail and with astonishing detachment. In view of this, Szyrocki's theory, albeit gingerly presented, that the above sonnet may have had its origin in a hangover, seems the more untenable.

In conclusion, the abrupt question; the bold, provocative directness and vivid detail of opening phrases that place the reader immediately at the heart of the matter; the rational analysis of the graphic scenes depicted; and the emotional reaction to what the mind has interpreted or comprehended are no less characteristic of Gryphius than they are of Donne, Herbert, or Southwell. They contribute, too, in large measure to that pictorially intense quality which Gerd Hemmerich notes in a brief article devoted, coincidentally, to a comparison of Donne and Gryphius—a quality which, he goes on to say, combines with a strikingly intellectual kind of imagery.[22] Such a blending of the two is remarkably reminiscent of the process of meditation.

The dissimilarities—religious, political, and literary—between England and the continent, and particularly between England and Germany, in the seventeenth century have caused serious problems for those seeking a synthesis of European literature under the general heading of Baroque. Nevertheless, it is quite clear that there does exist also a common European-English literary substratum

---

22. "Metaphysische Leidenschaft. Zur Lyrik von Andreas Gryphius und John Donne," *Text und Kritik* 7–8 (February 1965): 18–23.

based on shared traditions which extends back far before the seventeenth century. Certainly the art of formal meditation, practiced extensively throughout Europe, can be regarded as a significant strand of this common background. Having been so integral a part of daily life, meditation should be examined for its possible influence on literature. It is interesting to note that more than twenty years ago Werner Milch, after admonishing caution in any attempt to draw close and direct connections between German Baroque lyric and English metaphysical poetry, concluded nevertheless that a comparison of Donne and Herbert with Gryphius would be a valuable contribution.[23] A consideration of meditative poetry might serve as a beginning. It would be premature to suggest either that Gryphius was an adept at the practice of meditation or that his poetry was directly influenced by any of the practitioners or theoreticians of the discipline; indeed, their ideas and works were probably so well known as to preclude the demonstration of a clear relationship between the poet and any one author. On the other hand, it seems very possible that he did adapt various meditative methods and techniques to the creation of his poetry. Even a cursory review of the poems appears to offer enough evidence to warrant a more thorough investigation of the subject.

23. "Deutsche Barocklyrik und 'Metaphysical Poetry' in England," *Trivium* 5 (1947): 65–73.

# 10

## Toward a New Perspective

It would be presumptuous, on the basis of an examination of some few sonnets, to attempt any kind of systematic analysis or general evaluation of Gryphius' lyric poetry. Indeed, as was stated in the introduction, such was not the purpose of these studies. Yet even within the few poems considered here, images and ideas recur with such consistency and force that one can hardly help making a few general comments in summary. In Gryphius' lyric, man appears as a helplessly passive being, assailed from without by active negative forces while desperately seeking a firmer hold on his existence in a world whose component parts seem too illusory, too transitory, too deceptive for him to be really able to hold fast. Above all, it is continuity that is lacking. Gryphius seeks this continuity, a kind of permanence, in the moment, paradoxically the symbol of the very fragmentation that plagues him. The most reassuring example of that continuity, however, and of man's being a part of it is also a moment, that of Christ's birth. In this moment, not only does the Divine become one with man, who is then imbued with something of the Divine, but also a jealous God of arbitrary vengeance becomes one with and assumes the features and tendencies of an infinitely merciful Divinity. And yet, to convince the poet, it seems, this union must be brought about once more by the peculiar magic of the poetic word, for the merciful God often seems far removed, indeed, despite the claims of Christian dogma for his nearness and sympathetic participation in the affairs of this world.

A closer study of the aims, methods, and achievements of Gryphius' poetry, one which will work closely with and from the poems themselves, is still needed, in spite of the advances so recently made in this direction by the work of Jöns and by the more general study of Baroque imagery by Manfred Windfuhr,[1] as well as by the promise of Krummacher's book (soon to appear) on Gryphius' religious lyric.[2] Modern scholarship has already repeatedly acknowledged the undeniable debt of the Baroque poets to a largely uninterrupted flow of the principles and practice of classical rhetoric, whose influence is easily detected in their writing. It has also established, seemingly incontestably, these poets' lack of concern with "originality" and, generally, with the direct expression of their own personal condition, their innermost state of being. We have, however, Szyrocki perhaps to the contrary, reached the point in our critical investigations where we must go beyond indicating "deficiencies" in the poetry, as seen from the point of view of our modern sensibilities, and beyond decrying its evident failure to conform to our own current literary conventions. Rather than simply attempting to judge the poetry by current theories of what poetry should be, the critic must finally come to grips with it on its own terms, treating it on its own merits. He must certainly go beyond enumerating countless rhetorical minutiae and implying that these devices have been employed merely mechanically and without regard for the entirety of the poems involved. The criticism needed now would not discount in any way a poet's debt, as revealed in his works, to traditions long since established; it would, however, strive to return to some kind of balance in methods of criticism and approaches to poetry. Without some such attempt at new directions in Gryphius criticism, such unfortunate situations as Haile's dismay at the "triumph" of the representative formula over the "personal" in the revised "Es ist alles eitell," Schoolfield's apparent misunderstanding of just what Gryphius is about in

1. *Die barocke Bildlichkeit und ihre Kritiker* (Stuttgart, 1966).
2. Hans-Henrik Krummacher, *Der junge Gryphius und die Traditionen der Perikopen- und Passionsauslegung. Studien zur geistlichen Lyrik im 17. Jahrhundert* (München, in preparation).

"Abend," and Szyrocki's never-ending search for personal and subjective overtones as the most decisive evidence for the superiority
of the earliest versions of the lyrics will be multiplied yet many
times over.

In her book on Elizabethan and metaphysical imagery, Rosemond Tuve discusses at length the obstacles placed in the path of
understanding the poetry of both periods by applying to it inflex-
ibly rigid modern critical criteria: "Certainly both Elizabethan and
seventeenth-century poetry or the complete work of a single poet
in either time bulges out on all sides if we try to force it into the
narrow pattern defined by modern criteria. If it slips from the level
of the concrete to that of abstraction and of statement—as it constantly does—it offends one critic; if it loses sensuous immediacy in a
labyrinthine rhetorical patterning, it offends another; where it
speaks to the Will, it will offend a third, and, in all probability, lose
its power to unify the adult modern sensibilities of a fourth; in that
it habitually (and seemingly without regret) sacrifices rich texture
for clear logical structure I do not see how it can fail to fall out of
the line of vision of yet another."[3] And certainly the modern critic's
penchant for the personal, for the communication by the poet of his
inner feelings, has had its effect on the treatment of seventeenth-
century German poetry as well. One wonders whether the verdicts
on the revised "Es ist alles eitell" would have been quite so harsh
had the poet not been "caught in the act" of "depersonalization" by
the discovery at the turn of this century of the 1637 original and the
shift from "Ich seh'" to "Du sihst." With this stress on the personal,
the individual, and the concrete in poetry comes a disdain of generalization and the abstract. One looks askance at imagery which is
"borrowed" rather than created by the poet for a given poem. The
result is likely to be viewed as an unfeeling objectivization of language, a practice whereby the poet, no creator, may simply busy
himself with the secondary task of slightly varying images, the
meaning and function of which have already been firmly established. It is a process which is considered as little more than a kind
of intellectual playing with hollow words. Gerhard Fricke, for example, discusses Gryphius' frequent use of the allegorical ocean
voyage: "So liegt . . . schon seit Seneca die allegorische Bestimmtheit
des Bildes von der Seefahrt ganz fest. Alle entscheidenden Punkte

3. *Elizabethan and Metaphysical Imagery: Renaissance Poetic and
Twentieth-Century Critics* (Chicago, 1947).

sind in ihrer sinnbildlichen Bedeutsamkeit gültig durchhellt: Immer besagt das Meer das irdisch-zeitliche Dasein, das Schiff die menschliche Existenz . . . der Hafen die Errettung und häufig das Ende der Lebensfahrt, den Tod." ("Thus . . . since the time of Seneca, the allegorical determination of the image of the ocean voyage has been fixed. All decisive points have been explained once and for all in their emblematic significance: The sea always represents earthly-temporal existence, the ship, human existence . . . the harbor, rescue, and frequently the end of the voyage of life, death.") Variations, Fricke goes on to say, can be brought about within this basically predetermined total image only by shifts in accent, "etwa ob der Tod erwünscht ist oder ob er unvermutet und beklagenswert kommt, ob die Gefahr überwunden, ob geschicktes Lavieren empfohlen wird, ob der Nachdruck auf der Schilderung der Not und des Unglücks liegt usf" ("as, for example, the question of whether death is yearned for or comes unexpected and is to be lamented, whether the danger is overcome, whether skillful maneuvering is needed, whether the emphasis is to lie on the depiction of misery and unhappiness, and so forth").[4] And yet, with the sensitive touch of a great poet, Gryphius is able to endow altogether familiar symbols and traditional images with new power and life.

In the eyes of many, an emphasis on technique and rhetoric leads inevitably to poetic sterility, to an unseemly coldness, and, ultimately, to artificial, unfunctional ornament in place of imagery that is alive and warm. To a great extent, such has been the reaction in the past to Gryphius' poetry. On this matter we can do no better than to quote Miss Tuve: "Emphasis on technique does not produce 'ornament for ornament's sake'; foolish technicians who have nothing to say by means of the technique produce it. The Elizabethan period exhibits the normal number of foolish writers."[5] I would submit that the same is true of seventeenth-century German poetry.

4. *Die Bildlichkeit,* pp. 217–18.
5. Tuve, p. 48.

# Bibliography

Bekker, Hugo. "Gryphius as a Poet Between the Times." Unpublished paper read at the Annual Meeting of the Modern Language Association, December, 1962.

Benz, Richard. *Deutsches Barock.* Stuttgart, 1949.

Blume, Bernhard. "Die Kahnfahrt. Ein Beitrag zur Motivgeschichte des 18. Jahrhunderts," *Euphorion* 81 (1957): 355–84.

———. "Das Bild des Schiffbruchs in der Romantik," *Jahrbuch der deutschen Schillergesellschaft* 2 (1958): 145–61.

———. "Lebendiger Quell und Flut des Todes," *Arcadia* 1 (1966): 18–30.

———. "Rilkes 'Spätherbst in Venedig.'" In *Interpretationen I. Deutsche Lyrik von Weckherlin bis Benn,* pp. 277–90. Ed. Jost Schillemeit. Frankfurt am Main and Hamburg, 1965.

Böckmann, Paul. *Formgeschichte der deutschen Dichtung.* Hamburg, 1949.

Bright, John. *The Kingdom of God.* Nashville, 1952.

Burckhardt, Sigurd. "Zur Theorie der werkimmanenten Deutung." In *Festschrift für Bernhard Blume,* pp. 9–28. Ed. Egon Schwarz, Hunter G. Hannum, and Edgar Lohner. Göttingen, 1967.

Clark, Robert T., Jr. "Gryphius and the Night of Time." In *Wächter und Hüter. Festschrift für Hermann J. Weigand,* pp. 56–66. Ed. Curt von Faber du Faur, Konstantin Reichards, and Heinz Bluhm. New Haven, 1957.

Conradt, Edelgard. "Barocke Thematik in der Lyrik des Andreas Gryphius," *Neophilologus* 40 (1956): 99–117.

Conrady, Karl Otto. *Lateinische Dichtungstradition und deutsche Lyrik des 17. Jahrhunderts.* Bonner Arbeiten zur deutschen Literatur, vol. 4. Bonn, 1962.

Croce, Benedetto. *Der Begriff des Barock. Die Gegenreformation. Zwei Essays.* Zürich, 1925.

Curtius, Ernst Robert. *Europäische Literatur und lateinisches Mittelalter*, 2d ed. Bern, 1954.

Cysarz, Herbert. *Deutsche Barockdichtung*. Leipzig, 1924.

de Capua, A. G. "Two Quartets: Sonnet Cycles by Andreas Gryphius," *Monatshefte* 59 (1967): 325–29.

de Sales, St. Francis. *Introduction to the Devout Life*. Oxford and Cambridge, 1877.

Donne, John. *The Complete Poetry and Selected Prose of John Donne*. Ed. Charles M. Coffin. New York, 1952.

Eliade, Mircea. *Images and Symbols. Studies in Religious Symbolism*. Trans. Philip Mairet. New York, n.d.

Ermatinger, Emil. *Barock und Rokoko in der deutschen Dichtung*. Leipzig, 1926.

Faber du Faur, Curt von. "Andreas Gryphius. Der Rebell," *PMLA* 74 (1959): 14–27.

Fischer, Albert, ed. *Das deutsche evangelische Kirchenlied des 17. Jahrhunderts*. Gütersloh, 1904.

Fleming, Paul. *Paul Flemings deutsche Gedichte*. Ed. J. M. Lappenberg, 2 vols. In Bibliothek des literarischen Vereins in Stuttgart, vol. 82. Darmstadt, 1865.

Flemming, Willi. "Die Auffassung des Menschen im siebzehnten Jahrhundert," *Deutsche Vierteljahrsschrift* 6 (1928): 403–46.

————. *Der Wandel des deutschen Naturgefühls vom 15. zum 18. Jahrhundert*. Halle/Saale, 1931.

————. *Andreas Gryphius. Eine Monographie*. Stuttgart, 1965.

————. *Deutsche Kultur im Zeitalter des Barock*. Potsdam, 1937–1939.

Forster, Leonard. *The Temper of Seventeenth Century German Literature*. London, 1952.

Freeman, Rosemary. *English Emblem Books*. London, 1948.

Fricke, Gerhard. *Die Bildlichkeit in der Dichtung des Andreas Gryphius*. Berlin, 1933.

Friederich, Werner Paul. "From Ethos to Pathos: The Development from Gryphius to Lohenstein," *GR* 10 (1935): 223–36.

Friedrich, Hugo. *Epochen der italienischen Lyrik*. Frankfurt am Main, 1964.

Gode, Alexander, ed. *Anthology of German Poetry Through the Nineteenth Century*. New York, 1964.

Goethe, Johann Wolfgang von. *Goethes Werke*. Ed. Erich Trunz. Hamburg, 1948.

Gryphius, Andreas. *Andreas Gryphius. Werke in drei Bänden mit Ergänzungsband*. Ed. Hermann Palm. In Bibliothek des literarischen Vereins in Stuttgart, vols. 169–71. Unaltered photographic reprint of Tübingen edition, 1884. Hildesheim, 1961.

————. *Gesamtausgabe der deutschsprachigen Werke*, vols. 1–3. Ed. Marian Szyrocki and Hugh Powell. In Neudrucke deutscher Literaturwerke, n.s. vols 9–11. Tübingen, 1963–1965.

Gundolf, Friedrich. *Andreas Gryphius*. Heidelberg, 1927.

Haile, H. G. "The Original and Revised Versions of Two Early Sonnets by Andreas Gryphius: An Evaluation," *MLQ* 19 (1958): 307–18.

Hankamer, Paul. *Die Sprache, ihr Begriff und ihre Deutung im 16. und 17. Jahrhundert*. Bonn, 1927.

————. *Deutsche Gegenreformation und deutsches Barock. Die deutsche Literatur in Zeitraum des siebzehnten Jahrhunderts*. In Epochen der deutschen Literatur, geschichtliche Darstellungen, vol. 2, bk. 2. Stuttgart, 1947.

Heckel, H. *Geschichte der deutschen Literatur in Schlesien*. Breslau, 1929.

Heermann, Johann. *Johann Heermann*. Marburg, 1907.

Hemmerich, Gerd. "Metaphysische Leidenschaft. Zur Lyrik von Andreas Gryphius und John Donne," *Text und Kritik* 7–8 (February 1965): 18–23.

Hervey, James. "Meditations Among the Tombs." In *The Whole Works of the Late Reverend James Hervey, A.M. in Six Volumes*, vol. 1. Edinburgh, 1802.

Heusler, Andreas. *Deutsche Versgeschichte*, vol. 3. Berlin, 1956.

Hitzeroth, Carl. *Johann Heermann, ein Beitrag zur Geschichte der geistlichen Lyrik im siebzehnten Jahrhundert*. Marburg, 1907.

Hoerner, Margarete. "Gegenwart und Augenblick. Ein Beitrag zur Geistesgeschichte des 17. und 18. Jahrhunderts," *Deutsche Vierteljahrsschrift* 10 (1932): 457–77.

Hofacker, Erich. "Volkscharacter und Lyrik," *Monatshefte* 21 (1929): 188 ff.

Hübscher, Arthur. "Barock als Gestaltung antithetischen Lebensgefühls," *Euphorion* 24 (1922): 517–26, 759–805.

Hultsch, Paul. "Andreas Gryphius und die Mystik," *Schlesien* 5 (1960): 214–17.

Jöns, Dietrich Walter. *Das "Sinnen-Bild." Studien zur allegorischen Bildlichkeit bei Andreas Gryphius*. Stuttgart, 1966.

Junker, Christof. *Das Weltraumbild in der deutschen Lyrik von Opitz bis Klopstock*. Germanische Studien, no. 3. Berlin, 1932.

Just, Klaus Günther. "Andreas Gryphius und kein Ende?" *Schlesien* 10 (1965): 1–12.

Kayser, Wolfgang. *Geschichte des deutschen Verses*. Bern und München, 1960.

––––––. *Das sprachliche Kunstwerk. Eine Einführung in die Literaturwissenschaft*. Bern, 1948.

Klein, Johannes. *Geschichte der deutschen Lyrik, von Luther bis zum Ausgang des zweiten Weltkrieges*. Wiesbaden, 1957.

Koch, Ed. Emil. *Geschichte des Kirchenlieds und Kirchengesangs der christlichen insbesondere der deutschen Kirche*. Stuttgart, 1866–1876.

Krummacher, Hans-Henrik. "Andreas Gryphius und Johann Arndt. Zum Verständnis der 'Sonn- und Feiertags-Sonette.'" In *Formenwandel. Festschrift für Paul Böckmann*, pp. 116–37. Hamburg, 1964.

––––––. *Der junge Gryphius und die Traditionen der Perikopen- und Passionsauslegung. Studien zur geistlichen Lyrik im 17. Jahrhundert*. München (in preparation).

Langen, August. *Der Wortschatz des deutschen Pietismus*. Tübingen, 1954.

Lazarus, Gertrud. *Die kunstlerische Behandlung der Sprache bei Andreas Gryphius*. Hamburg, 1932.

Leighton, Joseph. "On the Interpretation of Andreas Gryphius's Sonnet 'Es ist alles eitel,'" *MLR* 60 (1965): 225–28.

Loyola, St. Ignatius. *The Spiritual Exercises of St. Ignatius Loyola, Spanish and English*. Ed. Joseph Rickaby, S.J. London, 1923.

Lüders, Eva. *Die Auffassung des Menschen im 17. Jahrhundert*. Düsseldorf, 1934.

Lüers, Grete. *Die Sprache der deutschen Mystik des Mittelalters im Werke Mechthilde von Magdeburg*. München, 1926.

Lunding, Erik. "Stand und Aufgaben der deutschen Barockforschung," *Orbis litterarum* 7 (1950): 27–91.

––––––. "Die deutsche Barockforschung. Ergebnisse und Probleme," *Wirkendes Wort* 2 (1951/52): 298–306.

Luther, Martin. *D. Martin Luthers Werke*, vols. 6, 11, *Die Deutsche Bibel*. Kritische Ausgabe. Weimar, 1929.

Mainusch, Herbert. "Dichtung als Nachahmung. Ein Beitrag zum Verständnis der Renaissancepoetik," *GRM* 41 (1960): 122–38.

Manheimer, Victor. *Die Lyrik der Andreas Gryphius*. Berlin, 1904.

Martz, Louis. *The Poetry of Meditation*. New Haven, 1965.

Milch, Werner. "Deutsche Barocklyrik und 'Metaphysical Poetry' in England," *Trivium* 5 (1947): 65–73.

Mönch, Walter. "Gongora und Gryphius," *Romanische Forschungen* 65 (1953/54): 300–316.

——. *Das Sonett. Gestalt und Geschichte*. Heidelberg, 1954.

Mourgues, Odette de. *Metaphysical Baroque and Précieux Poetry*. Oxford, 1953.

Müller, Günther. *Deutsche Dichtung von der Renaissance bis zum Ausgang des Barock*. Wildpark-Potsdam, 1927–1929.

Mützell, Julius, ed. *Geistliche Lieder der evangelischen Kirche aus dem 17. und der 1. Hälfte des 18. Jahrhunderts von Dichtern aus Schlesien und den umliegenden Landschaften verfaßt*, vol. 1. Braunschweig, 1858.

Naumann, Walter. *Traum und Tradition in der deutschen Lyrik*. Stuttgart, 1966.

Nelson, Lowry. *Baroque Lyric Poetry*. New Haven and London, 1961.

Newald, Richard. *Die deutsche Literatur von Späthumanismus zur Empfindsamkeit, 1570–1750*. In Geschichte der deutschen Literatur, vol 5. Ed. H. DeBoor and R. Newald. München, 1951.

Ohly, Friedrich. "Vom geistigen Sinn des Wortes im Mittelalter," *ZfdA* 89 (1958/59): 1–23.

Opitz, Martin. *Buch von der deutschen Poeterei*. Neudrucke deutscher Literaturwerke des 16. und 17. Jahrhunderts, no. 1. Halle, 1882.

——. *Weltliche und geistliche Dichtung*. In Deutsche Nationalliteratur, vol. 27. Ed. D. Desterley. Berlin and Stuttgart, n.d.

Peterson, Douglas L. "John Donne's *Holy Sonnets* and the Anglican Doctrine of Contrition," *Studies in Philology* 56 (1959): 504–18.

Pfeiffer, Johannes. "Andreas Gryphius als Lyriker." In *Zwischen Dichtung und Philosophie*, pp. 30–43. Bremen, 1947.

Platel, M. *Vom Volkslied zum Gesellschaftslied. Zur Geschichte des Liedes im 16. und 17. Jahrhundert*. Bern/Leipzig, 1939.

Powell, Hugh. "Andreas Gryphius and the 'New Philosophy,'" *German Life and Letters* 5 (1951/52): 274–78.

——. "Probleme der Gryphius Forschung," *Germanisch-Romanische Monatsschrift* n.s. 71, o.s. 38 (1957): 328–43.

——, ed. *Andreas Gryphius, Carolus Stuardus*. Leicester, 1955.

Praz, Mario. *Studies in Seventeenth-Century Imagery*, 2 vols. Studies of the Warburg Institute, no. 3. London, 1947.

Rehm, Walther. *Der Todesgedanke in der deutschen Dichtung vom Mittelalter bis zum Romantik*. Halle/Saale, 1928.

Rüttenauer, Isabella. "Die Angst des Menschen in der Lyrik des Andreas Gryphius." In *Aus der Welt des Barock*, pp. 36–55. Stuttgart, 1957.

Schöffler, Herbert. *Deutscher Osten im deutschen Geist von Martin Opitz zu Christian Wolff*. Frankfurt am Main, 1940.

Schoolfield, George. "Motion and Landscape in the Sonnets of Andreas Gryphius," *Monatshefte* 42 (1950): 341–46.

Schöne, Albrecht. *Säkularisation als sprachbildende Kraft. Studien zur Dichtung deutscher Pfarrersöhne*. Palaestra, no. 226. Göttingen, 1958.

———. *Emblematik und Drama im Zeitalter des Barock.* München, 1964.
Sommerfeld, Martin, ed. *Deutsche Barocklyrik.* Berlin, 1934.
Strich, Fritz. "Der europäische Barock." In *Der Dichter und die Zeit,* pp. 73–131. Bern, 1947.
Strutz, Adolf. *Andreas Gryphius. Die Weltanschauung eines deutschen Barockdichters.* Leipzig, 1931.
Szyrocki, Marian. *Der junge Gryphius.* Neue Beiträge zur Literaturwissenschaft, vol. 9. Berlin, 1959.
———. *Andreas Gryphius. Sein Leben und Werk.* Tübingen, 1964.
Tieck, Ludwig. *Ludwig Tiecks ausgewählte Werke in acht Bänden,* vol. 8. Ed. Heinrich Welti. Stuttgart, 1886.
Tillyard, E. M. W. *The Elizabethan World Picture.* New York, n.d.
Trunz, Erich. "Weltbild und Dichtung im deutschen Barock." In *Aus der Welt des Barock,* pp. 1–35. Stuttgart, 1957.
———. "Es ist alles eitel." In *Die deutsche Lyrik,* vol. 1, pp. 145–51. Ed. Benno von Wiese. Düsseldorf, 1959.
———. "Fünf Sonette des Andreas Gryphius." In *Vom Geist der Dichtung.* *Gedächtnisschrift für Robert Petsch,* pp. 180–205. Ed. F. Martini. Hamburg, 1949.
Tuve, Rosemond. *Elizabethan and Metaphysical Imagery: Renaissance Poetic and Twentieth-Century Critics.* Chicago, 1947.
Viëtor, Karl. *Probleme der deutschen Barockliteratur.* Leipzig, 1928.
———. "Vom Stil und Geist der deutschen Barockdichtung," *Germanisch-Romanische Monatsschrift* 14 (1926).
Wageman, Frederick Herbert. *Magic and Natural Science in German Baroque Literature.* New York, 1942.
Weber, Albrecht. "*Lux in tenebris lucet.* Zu Andreas Gryphius' 'Über die Geburt Jesu,' " *Wirkendes Wort* 7 (1956/57): 13–16.
Wehrli, Max. "Andreas Gryphius und die Dichtung der Jesuiten," *Stimmen der Zeit* 90, no. 1 (1964): 25–39.
Weisbach, Werner. *Der Barock als Kunst der Gegenreformation.* Berlin, 1921.
Wellek, René and Austin Warren. *Theory of Literature.* New York, 1949.
Wentzlaff-Eggebert, Friedrich Wilhelm. *Dichtung und Sprache des jungen Gryphius.* Berlin, 1936.
Weydt, Günther. "Sonettkunst des Barock. Zum Problem der Umarbeitung bei Andreas Gryphius," *Jahrbuch der deutschen Schillergesellschaft* 9 (1965): 1–32.
Willey, Basil. *The Seventeenth Century Background.* Cambridge, 1934.
Windfuhr, Manfred. *Die barocke Bildlichkeit und ihre Kritiker.* Stuttgart, 1966.
Wolfskehl, Marie L. *Die Jesusminne in der Lyrik des deutschen Barock.* In Giessener Beiträge zur deutschen Philologie, nos. 34–35. Giessen, 1934.
Ziemendorff, Ingeborg. *Die Metapher bei den weltlichen Lyrikern des deutschen Barock.* In Germanische Studien, no. 135. Berlin, 1933.